M000012073

EXPERIENCING
the MASS

Drawing Meaning from the
Five Moments of Mystery

© 2012 Saint Meinrad Archabbey
Written by Father David M. Knight
Published by Abbey Press
1 Hill Drive, St. Meinrad, IN 47577
All rights reserved.
Library of Congress Catalog Number 2010917381
ISBN 978-0-87029-452-5
Printed in the United States of America

EXPERIENCING
the MASS

Drawing Meaning from the
Five Moments of Mystery

by Father David M. Knight

✠ ABBey Press Publications
1 Hill Drive
St. Meinrad, IN 47577

TABLE OF CONTENTS

Introduction: *The Invitation*

*The acclamations and the responses of the faithful
to the [presider's] greetings and prayers
constitute that level of active participation that the
gathered faithful are to contribute in every form of the Mass,
so that the action of the entire community
may be clearly expressed and fostered.*

*The Christian faithful who gather together as one
to await the Lord's coming are instructed by the Apostle Paul to
sing together psalms, hymns, and spiritual songs.
Singing is the sign of the heart's joy.
Thus Saint Augustine says rightly, "Singing is for one who loves."
There is also the ancient proverb:
"One who sings well prays twice."
Great importance should therefore be attached to the use of
singing in the celebration of the Mass.*

*The gestures and posture of ... the people, ought to contribute
to making the entire celebration resplendent with beauty and
noble simplicity, so that the true and full meaning of the
different parts of the celebration is evident
and that the participation of all is fostered.
Therefore, attention should be paid to
what ... serves the common spiritual good of the People of God,
rather than private inclination or arbitrary choice.*[1]

The new *Roman Missal* is now in use in the Church. Some like,
some dislike the new translation. The real blessing of the new missal
is that it provides a wonderful new incentive to *pay attention to the
words and gestures* of the Eucharistic celebration.

---

[1]*General Instruction on the Roman Missal*, 2002, nos. 35-42. I have substi-
tuted "presider" for "priest" in this *Instruction* because it is the preferred
terminology of Vatican Council II, and of the *Instruction* itself, although
neither is rigidly consistent. All the faithful are "priests" by Baptism and
exercise their priesthood at Mass. The role of the ordained priest or
"presbyter" is to *preside* over the assembly's communal action. Bishop
Patrick Dunn of Auckland, New Zealand, explains this in his book *Priesthood: A Re-Examination of the Roman Catholic Theology of the Presbyterate*:
Alba House, New York, 1990, pp. 109-110 and chapter XII.

Are you ever bored at Mass? Do you know any teenagers who are? The remedy to boredom is simple: pay attention to the words! And to the gestures. The words are exciting. The gestures are full of meaning. No one who pays attention to them will ever be bored at Mass again.

Promises, promises? Try it and see.

This book will immerse you in understanding and appreciation of the Mass.

This should be a mystical experience.

To have a "mystical experience" means to be aware of a mystery as real and impacting my life right now.

The *Introductory Rites* of the Mass are a mystical experience of *new identity* through the *relationship* with God that we announce and celebrate.

Mass and Baptism both immerse us in the same mystery: the mystery of our salvation. The mystery of dying and rising in Christ. The mystery of *becoming Christ* to live as his risen body on earth.

A mystery is a truth that "invites endless exploration."

First Impressions

You are walking into church for Mass. What are you feeling? Thinking about? What do you intend to do? Why are you here?

The very last thing you are thinking of may be in fact the very first thing the liturgy invites you to do at Mass: to *praise God.*

In our culture we don't spend much time praising God. We are efficiency-minded. Praise is fine, but it doesn't get much done (unless someone is running for election). If we are going to spend time with God (or "on" God), we prefer to spend it productively. Asking for what we need. Getting new ideas or better understanding from the Scripture readings and the homily. Socializing with people. Even taking up a collection!

At the very lowest level of participation at Mass, we find some practical value: we are at least "fulfilling our obligation" of Sunday worship. That actually means a whole lot, if we think about the reasons behind it and what it says of us as persons and as believers.

"Fulfilling our obligation" does have practical value, and many people are willing to give the time to Mass just to "get it done."

But very few go to Mass to praise God. At least, that is the impression one gets.

"IT IS RIGHT TO GIVE YOU THANKS AND PRAISE."

The word *Eucharist* actually means "thanksgiving." Thanksgiving is a form of praise. If we have nothing to thank God for, we are hardly inclined to praise him. So the liturgy starts by inviting us to praise and thank God for a number of specific things. Some are specifically Christian things.

Rather than say "invites us," let's say the liturgy "guides us through" expressions of praise and thanksgiving that focus us on what we should be aware of about God. And appreciate him for.

This means that if we don't let ourselves be guided—if we don't *follow*—we miss out on what the liturgy is trying to give us.

So the first thing we have to say about Mass is that it is a *communal prayer*. We don't go to Mass to "do our own thing." We go to *take part* in a communal expression of worship. We give ourselves, surrender ourselves, to what the group is doing. We let ourselves be guided as active parts of a whole.

My father, a Baptist, went to Mass with me one time and remarked when he came out, "It's a dance, isn't it? It's all choreographed!"

In those days he was probably focused mostly on what the priest and others in the sanctuary were doing. But it was true of the congregation as well, who stood, sat, and knelt "on cue," and chimed in as a chorus when it was time for them to make responses. He gave me an insight I've never forgotten.

Unfortunately, not everyone in our congregations is as conscious of this as my father was. They do "go through the motions" dutifully, but many hardly seem to have their hearts in it. They are not enthusiastically "part of the dance." They know the basic steps, but they don't give any indication of hearing the music.

That is what these reflections hope to remedy. It is my hope that everyone who reads them will be better able to "follow" the Mass.

Will be personally "in tune" with its developing movements, and listening for the signals that indicate a change of focus, of pace, of mystery being expressed. I want to help people listen to the music and dance!

Dance, then, wherever you may be.
"I am the Lord of the Dance," said he.
"And I'll lead you all, wherever you may be.
"And I'll lead you all in the Dance, said he.[2]

A CONFESSION

Let's not underestimate the difficulty of dancing. Some people are too hung-up, too self-conscious to dance. Some are too hung-up to sing. The back pews at every Mass are filled with them. Some are too uptight to reveal any thoughts or feelings at all that they consider personal; they won't even express devotion to God. I understand this.

During a National Cursillo Encounter at Niagara Falls University I arrived late at an impromptu party in the student lounge. Everyone was singing folk songs. I love to sing, so I joined right in. But then they started to dance.

Everyone held hands in a long line and began snaking through the room. I couldn't join in. People were physically trying to pull me into the line, while I stubbornly held onto the bar—all the time saying to myself, "What is the matter with you? Why won't you get into the dance? You are just too hung-up!" But I couldn't join in.

The next Sunday I was back at my parish yelling at the silent spectators in the pews, "Why won't you sing?!!"

A voice behind me quietly asked, "Why won't you dance?"

The truth is, self-expression is dying to self. In varying degrees of spontaneity. It is letting go, losing oneself in a group, giving up control, becoming vulnerable. All self-revelation is.

To join in any communal self-expression is to give up some of your autonomy. You stop being just an individual doing your individual thing. You begin doing what the group is doing, even if it is just

[2]Text: Sydney Carter, © 1963, Steiner & Bell, Ltd. (Hope Publishing Co.)

singing a song. Then you become a part in a whole. This is a true *dying* to self. Jesus said it: to become "one bread" each grain must die:

> Very truly, I tell you, unless a grain of wheat falls into the earth and dies, it remains just a single grain; but if it dies, it bears much fruit.[3]

A FUNDAMENTAL CHOICE

Before you begin to read these reflections on the Mass, you first need to decide whether you accept the Mass at all. Do you accept communal worship of God? Do you accept to worship as part of a whole? To "join in," listen to the music, follow the steps, get into the dance?

To put this in legalistic language, are you willing to participate in Eucharist according to the guidelines spelled out in the Church's *General Instruction for the Roman Missal*? When giving God thanks and praise, are you willing to let yourself be *guided* by the liturgical rules—knowing that, more than just "rules," they are the Church's expressed and embodied insight into what the Eucharistic celebration is? They do more than tell us what to do; they explain to us what we are doing. So will you participate in Mass as a Catholic?

Let us be clear from the outset. The Mass is participation in a sacrifice. To celebrate Eucharist is to take part, personally and communally, in the sacrifice of Jesus on the cross, which in the Mass is remembered and made present. In every Mass we accept to die with and in Christ on the cross, as we did on the day of our Baptism. With him and in him we "offer our flesh" for the life of the world, saying in communion with him on the cross, to every member of the human race, "This is my body, given up for you."

This takes us into a level of mystery that we will not explicitly address until the fourth theme of this series, which deals with the *Eucharistic Prayer*. But it is enough to encourage us, here and now, to make the sacrifice of "losing ourselves" in communal expression in order to "find ourselves" as part of a community at Mass. Then, when the presider invites us, "Let us give thanks to the Lord our God," we can answer sincerely, "*It is right and just* to give him thanks and praise."

This begins with the *Introductory Rites*.

---

[3] *John* 12:24.

The Introductory Rites

The First Moment of Mystery:
Our Christian Identity

"Our Father, who art in heaven...."

*The purpose of the Introductory Rites is to ensure that the faithful
who come together as one, establish communion
and dispose themselves to ... celebrate the Eucharist worthily.*

*For in the celebration of Mass,
in which the Sacrifice of the Cross is perpetuated
Christ is really present
in the very liturgical assembly gathered in his name,
in the person of the minister, in his word,
and indeed substantially and continuously under the
Eucharistic species.*[1]

The first of the five *promises* of Baptism is a *new identity*. This
identity is the first of the five *mysteries* of Baptism: we *become
Christ*, true children of the Father, recipients of the "gift of the Holy
Spirit." This first mystery and promise is presented from the outset
in the *Introductory Rites* of the Mass.[2]

Most celebrations begin with some form of *identification*. When
we announce what we are celebrating, we also declare who we are.

"Happy Fourth of July" tells us we are all people who cherish inde-
pendence. "Merry Christmas!" says we are people, whether Christians
or not, who celebrate the birth of Jesus. "Welcome to the birthday
party of...." identifies us as family or friends who appreciate this
particular person's existence.

---

[1]*General Instruction on the Roman Missal*, 2002, nos. 27, 46.
[2]See the *Catechism of the Catholic Church*, not only 1265, but the whole
section on the "Grace of Baptism," 1262-1274. This is not complete without
the section on "The Church—Body of Christ," nos. 787-801.

We begin the Eucharistic Celebration *"In the name of the Father, and of the Son, and of the Holy Spirit."* The cross we trace on our bodies and the words we speak tell us both what we are celebrating and who we are.

> When we cross ourselves, let it be with a real sign of the cross. Instead of a small cramped gesture that gives no notion of its meaning, let us make a large unhurried sign, from forehead to breast, from shoulder to shoulder, consciously feeling how it includes the whole of us, our thoughts, our attitudes, our body and soul, every part of us at once. How it consecrates and sanctifies us.[3]

We are the people who, when we worship God, "look up to heaven" as most people do. We even raise our hand toward heaven as we begin the *Sign of the Cross.* But then we do something different. We put our hand *on our forehead*, on our head, to say we *know* him. And we call him "Father."

We are the people who *know God* and call him "Father." We begin the Mass by declaring ourselves his children.

SONS AND DAUGHTERS OF THE FATHER

We are God's children literally; not just in a loose sense, as some call all humans "children of God." That is a metaphor. Creatures are not the same thing as children. We are not created children of God. We have to be reborn "of water and Spirit" to be that. Then we are called God's "adopted" children, since Jesus is the "only begotten Son of God." But "adopted" is a misleading term here.[4]

It does not refer just to juridical or "legal" adoption, even though one's "adoptive" parents are one's real parents. God is not our father just because he nurtures us, provides for us, teaches and forms us, and is committed to us as extensively and irrevocably as a father is. When we call God our Father, we mean he has made us *sharers in his own divine life.*

By creation God gave us created life, human life. But when we are "reborn," he shares with us his own unique Life as God, uncreated Life, eternal Life, Life without beginning or end; divine Life.

---

[3]Romano Guardini, *Sacred Signs*, tr. Grace Branham, © 1956 by Pio Decimo Press, St. Louis, Mo.
[4]*John 3:5; Matthew 3:11.*

It is as if someone, by "adopting" a puppy, could give the puppy human life, make it live by the owner's own, personal human life.

Even God could not do this, because the puppy could not become human without losing its nature, ceasing to be a dog. But humans can "become God" by sharing in God's own life without ceasing to be human, because our natures are already "in the image" of God. Our natures were designed to know and love, which is what God does. So when God lets us know and love as he does, by sharing in his life, we are not doing something totally foreign to what we were designed to do, and our "human nature" is not changed. We still know and love, which is according to our nature, but these operations are "elevated." We know and love now on the level of God, by sharing in his own act of knowing and loving.

This makes us more truly, more deeply, more "really" God's children than we are the children of our parents. We are "children of the Father" in a way that defines our "being" even more than being children of our biological or adoptive parents defines us.

That is the deep, the divine mystery of who we are. We announce it in the first words that begin the Mass: *"In the name of the Father!"*

It is what we are reminded of when we pray, *"Our Father, who art in heaven...."*

Is this exciting or not?

We Are *Filii in Filio*: "in the Son"

In the Sign of the Cross, when we say *"...and of the Son,"* we bring our hand *down* from our forehead and place it on our heart. This is our profession of faith that God the Son came down, as Jesus, in the Incarnation—not just to be *Emmanuel*—"God-with-us," but to incorporate us into his own body by Baptism, so that now he lives in us and we in him. This is the "mystery" of our identity as Christians. Paul said he was sent to preach "the riches of the glory of *this mystery*, which is *Christ in you*, the hope of glory." Each one of us says now with Paul, in recognition of the effect of Baptism, "It is no longer I who live, but *it is Christ who lives in me*."[5]

---

[5]*Colossians* 1:27; *Galatians* 2:20. See *John* 15:1-8.

11

This is one Scriptural source for the foundational Christian affirmation that by Baptism we have "become Christ." This means that when we walk into church and look around at Mass, we should be conscious that everyone we see has "become Christ." And in each one Christ has become a man, a woman, a child, American, Vietnamese, Hispanic, old or young, healthy or sick, outstanding or unexceptional, a moral "straight arrow," or a broken and struggling backslider.

The point is, we are all Christ, and in all of us Christ has become what we are, even claiming as his own our human imperfections in every way possible without being personally guilty of our sins.[6]

We know that on the cross Jesus was made to "be sin" by taking us, with all of our sins, into his own body. Although in his own person he "knew no sin," as one with us he knew the shame of every sin that would ever be committed. And he knew it as his own: our sins were the sins of his own flesh. Taking them down to the grave "in him," he annihilated them, so that "in him" we might rise as a "new creation," having "become the righteousness of God."[7]

In the eternal "now" of God, our purification is an accomplished fact. But in the ongoing before-and-after of present, earthly time, we can say that Jesus is still "made sin" in all the members of his body whose flesh he calls his own. These, with all of their sins, are the people we see around us at Mass. In them we recognize Jesus.

And in them we accept Jesus. We accept Jesus as them, and them as Jesus, or we don't accept Jesus at all.

Would we be passing "from the sublime to the ridiculous" if we urged this as a reason for *sitting together* at Mass? Or would we just be bringing faith down to earth? By common custom, Catholic congregations at Mass follow the "first law of gases": no matter how few or numerous, they occupy all available space. Except for family groups and special friends, they sit as far from one another as possible. What does this say about us?

First, it says we are not expressing recognition of *who we are*. If we are all "sons and daughters of the Father," are we not one family? Should we not sit together—all of us—as one family?

---

[6]See *Catechism of the Catholic Church*, no. 795.
[7]*2Corinthians* 5:15-21.

If we believe that all have "become Christ," shouldn't we want to sit next to Jesus? No protocol is involved here: at Mass, Jesus in one person is the equal of Jesus in every other. The only dignity anyone claims at Mass is divinity! We are all equally sinners and equally divine. Besides that, nothing really counts. So if we make distinctions between friends and strangers, rich and poor, the socially respected and despised, are we not failing to "recognize the body of the Lord"?

When Paul wrote that "whoever eats the bread or drinks the cup of the Lord in an unworthy manner will be answerable for the body and blood of the Lord," he was saying that if those present don't recognize *each other* as the "body of the Lord," and relate to each other accordingly, they are not "discerning the body," and they "eat and drink judgment against themselves."

Paul was denouncing the visible separation he saw within the Corinthian community: "I do not commend you, because ... to begin with, when you come together as a church, I hear that there are divisions among you." Would he not say the same to a parish today where there are wide gaps in the pews between one group and the next, while some people are sitting completely alone? If we feel that by sitting next to people we don't know we are "intruding on their space," we are saying we are not one family, much less one body. We are clearly, blatantly announcing that we do not feel sufficiently united in love to sit together as families and friends spontaneously do. This is to call down "judgment against ourselves." No one will believe we are worshipping together in the "communion of the Holy Spirit."[8]

ONE IN THE SPIRIT

We conclude the Sign of the Cross by adding, "...*and of the Holy Spirit.*" As we do, we move our hand from our heart to our shoulder, and then in a wide arc from one shoulder to the other. It is an arc meant to embrace the world.

We are saying that we who have Christ's love in our hearts, are impelled, *sent*, as his body, and in the power of his Spirit, to bring the whole world together into one family. Into the one body of Christ. Into the "peace and unity of his kingdom."

---

[8]See *New Jerome Biblical Commentary* (1990) on *1Corinthians* 11:17-34.

For the love of Christ urges us on, because we are convinced that one has died for all ... so that those who live might live no longer for themselves, but for him who died and was raised for them.

To do this, we must first be united ourselves—with God and one another—in the "communion of the Holy Spirit." This is no ordinary unity.[9]

The union we have with one another as Christians is not just a common agreement on "creed, code, and cult," a commitment to the same doctrines, rules, and religious practices. A "Catholic" is not someone who just keeps the Commandments, accepts the truths summarized in our "Profession of Faith," says recommended prayers, goes to Mass, and receives the sacraments regularly. That is not the mystery of "communion in the Holy Spirit" Paul writes about:

I beg you to lead a life *worthy of the calling* to which you have been called ... making every effort to maintain the *unity of the Spirit* in the bond of peace.

There is *one body and one Spirit*, just as you were called to the one hope of your calling, *one Lord, one faith, one baptism*, one God and Father of all, who is *above all and through all and in all.*[10]

If we pay attention to the words, what does this tell us?

"ONE LORD"

By "one Lord" we don't just mean someone we all obey. The "one Lord" is the awesome mystery proclaimed on Sinai:

Hear, O Israel: The LORD is our God, the LORD alone. You shall love the LORD your God with all your heart, and with all your soul, and with all your might.[11]

---

[9]*2Corinthians* 5:14 and13:14. The word translated as "communion" is *koinonia*. The previous translation was "fellowship, which we understand more readily but might confuse with a fellowship that is merely human. This fellowship is a mystery. It is a communal sharing in the divine life of God ("grace"). That means we are united with each other by sharing together in God's own act of knowing by *faith*, in God's own intentions by *hope*, in God's own act of self-giving by *love*. This is what we have in common.

[10]*Ephesians* 4:1-6

[11]*Deuteronomy* 6:4-5.

The "One Lord" is the God we cannot know or name except with the voice of the Holy Spirit sent into our hearts, crying, "Abba! Father!" As we mean the word, "no one can say, 'Jesus is Lord' except by the Holy Spirit." When we make the Sign of the Cross we proclaim ourselves a people united in a common experience of knowing the One God as "God, almighty Father"—knowing him as he can only be known by those who have received the gift of sharing in the life of the Son. This is "communion in the Holy Spirit." It is the communal experience of knowing the awesome mystery of the God who revealed himself to Abraham, Moses, and Elijah; and who "in these last days has spoken to us by a Son ... the reflection of God's glory and the exact imprint of God's very being."[12]

"ONE FAITH"

By "one faith" we don't mean just a common adherence to the same body of doctrines. The true meaning—and mystery—of "faith" is "the gift of *sharing in God's own act of knowing*. Faith is a divine light by which we see divine things. Without it the most brilliant human intellects are blind.

> No one comprehends what is truly God's except the Spirit of God. Now we have received not the spirit of the world, but the Spirit that is from God, so that we may understand the gifts bestowed on us by God. And we speak of these things in words not taught by human wisdom but taught by the Spirit, interpreting spiritual things to those who are spiritual.
>
> Those who are unspiritual do not receive the gifts of God's Spirit, for they are foolishness to them, and they are unable to understand them because they are spiritually discerned.[13]

Those who have experienced the difference between "learning" their religion and "seeing" the truths of faith are in the "communion of the Holy Spirit." When Paul asked for us to "be united in the same mind and the same purpose," he was speaking of more than human agreement on doctrines and goals. He was inviting us to surrender to the *mystery of enlightenment* by the Holy Spirit: "Let the same mind be in you that was in Christ Jesus." This is an agreement based

---

[12]*Galatians* 4:6; *Romans* 8:15-16; *1Corinthians* 12:3. For Abraham see *Genesis* 12:1; 15:12-18; 17:1-8. For Moses see *Exodus* 33:12 to 34:8. For Elijah see *1Kings* 19:9-13. For Jesus see *John* 1:1-18. *Hebrews* 1:1-3.
[13]*1Corinthians* 2:11-14. See *Matthew* 11:27.

15

not only on doctrine but on shared spiritual discernment. It was the common experience of the early Church.[14]

As Christians, we identify ourselves as people who have received the "gift of the Spirit," and who are united with each other in a common experience of that gift. This is the "communion (*koinonia*) of the Holy Spirit."[15]

"ONE BAPTISM"

These words return us to where we began and summarize all the rest. The real mystery of our unity is that by "becoming Christ" in Baptism, we have become one body, communally alive by sharing in the one divine Life of God. By our participation in his Life (grace) we can know the mystery of God as "Lord." And we know it by sharing in God's own knowledge of himself, which is "faith."

All this is ours because in Baptism we were incorporated into the body of Christ on the cross, died with and in him, and rose with him, and he in us, to be his risen body on earth.

That is why the identifying sign we make as Christians is the sign of the cross.

This is the mystery we celebrate and make present at Mass.

If we pay attention to the words, will we find the Sign of the Cross exciting?

---

[14] *1 Corinthians* 1:10; *Philippians* 2:5. See *Acts* 11:11-18; 13:4; 15:1-29; 16:6.
[15] See *John* 7:39; *Acts* 2:38; 8:15; 10:45; 19:1-6; *Galatians* 3:2; *Hebrews* 5:4.

QUESTIONS FOR REFLECTION AND DISCUSSION:

- Is there anything in this explanation you did not already know? Or were just not aware of?
- Do you think of the assembly as *identifying* itself at the beginning of Mass?
- Do you think that from now on you will be consciously identifying yourself as a Christian as Mass begins?
- Have you spent much time thinking about the meaning of the words in the Sign of the Cross?
- Are these thoughts exciting? Is the Sign of the Cross exciting to think about?
- What mysteries can you experience as real and impacting your life when you make the Sign of the Cross?
- Does this make the Mass more exciting?

The Greeting

When the Entrance chant is concluded, the [presider]...
together with the whole gathering, makes the Sign of the Cross.
Then he signifies the presence of the Lord to the community
gathered there by means of the Greeting.
By this Greeting and the people's response,
the mystery of the Church gathered together is made manifest.[1]

The grace of our Lord Jesus Christ,
and the love of God,
and the communion of the Holy Spirit
be with you all.

After the Sign of the Cross, the presider looks at the people and greets the people with the words above or with the shorter form that Paul used to begin all thirteen of the letters attributed to him: "*Grace to you and peace from God our Father and the Lord Jesus Christ.*" Or he may just say, "*The Lord be with you.*"[2]

We shouldn't just let these words slip by. The *Greeting* is a perfect example of the principle, "You will never be bored at Mass if you just *pay attention to the words.*" And notice the presider turns to look at the people as he says them. He is seeing and saying what they are.

What is the *"grace of our Lord Jesus Christ"*? I have asked this of gathered Christians innumerable times and never received a sure, precise answer. But these words should be so ingrained in our heads and hearts that just hearing them makes us vibrate all over. The "grace of our Lord Jesus Christ" is the *favor of sharing in the divine life of God.* That is exciting!

We begin the Mass announcing that we are divine! You are divine. The person next to you is divine. Does that give you something to think about or not?

---

[1]*General Instruction on the Roman Missal*, 2002, no. 50.
[2]The text under the title is the ending of *2Corinthians* 13:14. The liturgy makes it more personal by changing Paul's "the Lord" to "our Lord." There are slight modifications of the second greeting in three of Paul's letters.

We explained this mystery above. Here we just need to note that if we really listen to the *Greeting* it will define us and excite us at the same time. It is the Good News!

"And the love of God..." The Mass in French, Spanish, German, Portuguese, Italian, and Polish changes this to "the love of God the Father." That makes the *Greeting* explicitly Trinitarian. Here again, the words should make us vibrate. Haven't we all experienced the love of God? Do we think so often of the ways we have experienced his love that just hearing the words *"love of the Father"* sets us tingling?

Well, maybe not. But it should. And it can, if we let every Mass remind us to think back and remember his "great deeds" in our lives—and his "random acts of kindness." Love lives on remembering. The Mass is loaded with remembrance.

"And communion in the Holy Spirit..." We spent some time on this above. The presider is just reminding us that we are a faith community; an assembly united by shared faith, shared hope, shared love. We are here to experience the Holy Spirit, and to "manifest the gifts of the Spirit."

Now there are varieties of gifts, but the same Spirit;
and there are varieties of services, but the same Lord;
and there are varieties of activities, but it is the same God who activates all
of them in everyone.

To each is given the manifestation of the Spirit for the common good.[3]

The point is, there are no "silent spectators" at Mass. *Everyone* is there to minister. Everyone is there to make the Mass "happen" for themselves and others. And we do it in a variety of ways:—in all the ways we express our faith. Our hope. Our love. All the ways that reveal the presence of the Spirit in our hearts. For example:

The entrance hymn: This is the first pass-fail test that reveals whether we are intending to just "be at Mass" or to "celebrate Eucharist." Singing is a service. A gift of self.

Body language. Is mine as reverent as if I were in the sanctuary? In spite of architectural appearances, if the church were a theater, the sanctuary would not be the stage. The Mass is "theater in the

---

[3] *1Corinthians* 12:7.

round." Everyone in church is an actor, a player. There are no spectators except perhaps the "great a cloud of witnesses" in heaven by whom *Hebrews* says we are surrounded.[4]

Gestures. Do I genuflect or bow when I enter church? Do I *look* at Christ in the tabernacle when I do? When I make the Sign of the Cross, is my mind somewhere else? When I stand or sit, or kneel, am I consciously giving symbolic expression to an identified attitude? Do I make the Sign of the Cross on my forehead, lips, and breast as the minister does before reading the Gospel? Prayerfully? Whether I choose to receive Communion in my hand or on my tongue, do I know *why* I am making this choice? What I am saying by it?

The responses: When I join in the responses and "acclamations" as a member of the "chorus" when the congregation voices its union with the presider, do I sound like I mean what I am saying? Do I sound that way to my children? Do I mumble or proclaim?[5]

We could continue with examples, but these are enough to confront us with the basic choice: Do I want to participate in the "Eucharistic celebration" as a Catholic? This means giving that "full and active participation by all the people" that the bishops in the Second Vatican Council said was their "paramount concern" in the "restoration and development of the sacred liturgy."[6]

Active participation in the Mass, they said, is the "indispensable source from which the faithful are to derive the true Christian spirit." We have seen that proven by the distressing number of youth and adults who, feeling that they were not "getting anything" out of the Mass, have just stopped assembling with the Church.

For that reason, the Council said, pastors should "energetically set about achieving" this participation through "whatever formation is necessary." But it makes no difference what the pastors do, if the congregation won't cooperate.

That is a motive to take seriously this *book*. We are *all* called and consecrated by Baptism to be *ministers* and "priests" to one another.

---

[4]*Hebrews* 12:1.
[5]Vatican II lists these and other acts of participation in the *Constitution on the Sacred Liturgy*, no. 30.
[6]See *doc. cit.*, the *Constitution* ... nos. 11, 14, 17, 19, 21, 30, and 41.

If we don't accept to let the Spirit work actively in us at Mass for the good of all, when and where will we do it?[7]

All the bishops of the world, assembled at the Vatican Council, signed the statement:

> Mother Church earnestly desires that all the faithful be led to that *full, conscious and active participation* in liturgical celebrations which is demanded by the very nature of the liturgy. Such participation by the Christian people as "a chosen race, a royal priesthood, a holy nation..." is their right and duty by reason of their Baptism.

Does this united plea of the bishops animate me to really "get into" the Mass?

Do I find that prospect exciting?

"THE LORD BE WITH YOU"

There has been much discussion about the change the new Missal makes in the assembly's response to "The Lord be with you," which appears for the first time as the third optional *Greeting* in the Mass. Now, instead of responding, "And also with you," the people will answer, "And with your spirit."

Cardinal Jean-Marie Lustiger, deceased Archbishop of Paris, would say we are focusing on the wrong phrase! He would have us focus on the greeting instead of on the response. The actual words of greeting are just "The Lord with you."

Cardinal Lustiger prefers this *Greeting* to all the others, saying that it "sums up the whole history of salvation." In Latin, Greek, and Hebrew the wording is precisely and concisely, "*The Lord with you.*" This is the expression, he says, not of a *wish* but of a *fact*— "*non un souhait, mais un fait.*"

More than a wish, it is an act of faith, an affirmation which courses through all of Scripture, recognizing God unceasingly

---

[7]See the *Catechism of the Catholic Church*, no. 783: "Jesus Christ is the one whom the Father anointed with the Holy Spirit as Priest, Prophet, and King. The whole People of God participates in these three offices of Christ and bears the responsibilities for mission and service that flow from them."

present to his people: thus, *"with you."* It is the best of all blessings, for it is a condensed formulation of the Covenant God entered into with his people on Mount Sinai.

"The Lord with you" pronounces the Name of God revealed to Moses.... Whether we say in Latin *Dominus*, in Greek *Kyrios*, or in Hebrew *Adonai*, the divine Name means God is with us. It is the revelation, not only of the Being of God, but of the presence of God to his people. To say, *"The Lord with you"* is to affirm the core of God's Revelation: that God himself has covenanted to take up residence among his people. It is to renew, in hope and thanksgiving, the Covenant made through Moses.[8]

If we pay attention to the words, we will be led into depths of meaning that escape any particular translation. That is exciting!

QUESTIONS FOR REFLECTION AND DISCUSSION:

- What is "the grace of our Lord Jesus Christ"?
- What experiences have you had of the "love of God"?
- Do you feel "communion in the Holy Spirit" at Mass?
- What mysteries can you experience as real and impacting your life if you listen to the words of the *Greeting*?
- What more could you do to take that "full, conscious, active part" in the Mass that the bishops proclaim is your "right and duty"?

---

[8]*La Messe*, Bayard, 1988, pp. 56-57. See *Exodus* 3:14.

Penitential Act

Then the [presider] invites those present to take part in the
Act of Penitence, which, after a brief pause for silence,
the entire community carries out
through a formula of general confession....
On Sundays, especially in the Season of Easter,
in place of the customary Act of Penitence...
the blessing and sprinkling of water to recall Baptism may take place.[1]

I confess to almighty God
and to you, my brothers and sisters,
that I have greatly sinned....

At meetings of Alcoholics Anonymous, people introduce themselves by saying, "I am (first name only), and I am an alcoholic."

That levels the playing field. No one is there as "doctor, lawyer,
or Indian chief." Just as an alcoholic. Nothing else. That is the way
we introduce ourselves at Mass. As sinners, nothing else. The
presider has already identified us as divine children of the Father,
the living body of Jesus Christ, each of us a walking temple of the
Holy Spirit. We are conscious of all this.

But as we stand in the presence of God and others at Mass, we
choose to present ourselves simply as sinners. Everybody does. No
one is "holier than thou." There are no accepted and unaccepted. No
one should feel excluded or there with less right to celebrate than
any other. All, without exception—the presiding priest or bishop
included—are saying, "I have greatly sinned. In my thoughts and in
my words. In what I have done and in what I have failed to do." We
are all there as sinners. Without exception.

And no one is minimizing or making excuses. Each says, "What I
have done was through my fault. Yes, through my fault. Through my
most grievous fault."

That should make us all, even if we identify ourselves with the "tax
collectors and the prostitutes," feel at home. As indeed we should. The
Church—and the church building—is our home. No one can say we

---

[1]*General Instruction on the Roman Missal*, 2002, no. 51.

are unwelcome in our Father's house. No one has a greater right to be there than the people Jesus died for. Within the Church, "sinner" means "citizen." It means more than that. We will see it also means "family."[2]

Is this exciting? Is it a reason to "give God thanks and praise"?

KYRIE ELEISON

We begin the Mass declaring ourselves accepted and accepting. But the liturgy takes us another step into the mystery of God's love. Why are we accepted?

The root of it, of course, is just God's "steadfast love," which is Scripture's "virtual definition of God." It occurs 171 times in the Old Testament alone.[3] But there is another reason. We are acceptable to God because we are *family*.

We follow up the *Penitential Rite* by repeating after the presider the triple prayer, *Kyrie eleison, Christe eleison, Kyrie eleison*.

Presider: Lord, have mercy.   *People*: Lord, have mercy.
Presider: Christ, have mercy.   *People*: Christ, have mercy.
Presider: Lord, have mercy.   *People*: Lord, have mercy.

"Have mercy" does not just mean "Help!" Much less is it a terrified cringing under the upraised arm of a threatening God. Nor do we "have mercy" when we just give help to others because they are needy. The merest whiff of condescension in this is what moved St. Vincent de Paul to caution his Sisters, "Pray that the poor will forgive you the bread you give them!"

"Have mercy" is a translation of the Greek *eleison*. It is rooted in the Semitic word for a mother's womb. It means to come to the aid of another *out of a sense of relationship*. It carries the same weight as the foundational virtue of Roman culture—the *pietas* of *pius Aeneas* in the *Aeneid*—which referred to the "gut bond" of loyalty to family, friends, and fellow citizens, to the gods of hearth and homeland. This connection is explicit in the Spanish Mass, where "Have

---

[2]*Matthew* 21:31-32.
[3]See the *Jerome Biblical Commentary* (1968) on *John* 1:14.

mercy" is translated, "*Ten piedad.*" When Jesus taught us to "have mercy" on everyone in need, he extended *pietas* and "love of neighbor" to embrace the whole human race.

When we ask God to "have mercy," we are reminding him that he has made us family. We are his relatives. We address this prayer to Jesus as "Lord" and "Christ" ("Anointed") because it is "through him, with him, and in him" that we have become sons and daughters of the Father.

More: we are Jesus' own body. What Paul said of our relationship with other members of the body is true of our relationship with Jesus the head: "If one member suffers, all suffer together with it; if one member is honored, all rejoice together with it." It is out of awareness of his identification with us as members of his own body that we say to Jesus, "Have mercy." He suffers with us in our sinfulness. He rejoices with us in our purification. They are his.[4]

We were taught as children to say, when we saw someone suffering from poverty, sickness, or even sin: "There, but for the grace of God, go I." But this can have different meanings.

If I say these words when I see a homeless drunk panhandling on the sidewalk, I might be thinking: "Thanks be to God I am not a drunk." Then if I give him a dollar, that is not mercy. But if I myself am a recovering alcoholic, when I say "There but for the grace of God go I," it has a totally different meaning. I am seeing myself in the drunk on the street. I have been there. I am what he is—and only one drink away from winding up where he is. There is no feeling of superiority. Whatever help I give him will come from a sense of identification. Of relationship, not condescension. It will be "mercy."

When Jesus sees us in our sins, or suffering the consequences our free choices have brought upon us, he sees himself. On the cross he was "made sin" for us. He took us, with all our sins, into his own body, making our sins the sins of his own flesh. When he sees us, he says, "There *because* of the grace of God go I! I took their sins into myself. I became what they are. For their sake the Father made me to *be sin* who knew no sin, so that in me they might become the righteousness

---

[4] *1Corinthians* 12:26.

25

of God." He cannot despise us without despising himself on the cross. When he comes to our aid, it is out of a sense of identification with us. That is "mercy."[5]

Christ's identification with us and ours with him did not end on the cross. In his resurrection we rose "in him," a "new creation," having become, in him, "the very holiness of God."[6]

Is it any wonder that we exclaim with Paul, "Blessed be the God and Father of our Lord Jesus Christ, the Father of mercies"? We say to the Father during Mass: "You gave us your Son" to be made "one like ourselves,"—even taking our sins into himself—so that through our dying and rising with him in Baptism *you might see and love in us what you see and love in Christ.*"[7]

This is the true mystery of our relationship with Christ. Through the Baptism that made us one with him in his death and rising, we have become "the very holiness of God." We have *become Christ.* It is on the basis of that relationship that we ask God for "mercy." We come before the Father as identified with his Son. We come before Jesus as identified with himself.

> I will do *whatever you ask in my name,* so that the Father may be glorified in the Son. If *in my name* you ask me for anything, I will do it. On that day you will ask nothing of me. Very truly, I tell you, if you ask anything of the Father *in my name,* he will give it to you. Until now you have not asked for anything in my name. Ask and you will receive, so that your joy may be complete.[8]

The *Introductory Rites* celebrate the *new identity* we have through the Baptism by which we entered into the mystery of Christ's redemptive sacrifice on the cross. Is this, or is this not exciting? If only we *pay attention to the words.*

---

[5] *2Corinthians* 5:21.
[6] This is the translation of *2Corinthians* 5:21 in the 1970 *New American Bible.* For "new creation" see *2Corinthians* 5:17.
[7] See *2Corinthians* 1:3 and *Preface VII* for Sundays in Ordinary Time.
[8] *John* 14:13-14; 16:23-24.

QUESTIONS FOR REFLECTION AND DISCUSSION:

- Is the *Penitential Act* for you an "upper" or a "downer"?
- Does it give you joy that at Mass no one claims to be anything but a sinner? Does it make you proud of your Church?
- What is the difference between "having mercy" and just helping someone?
- On what relationship with the Father and with Jesus do we base our confidence when we ask for "mercy"?
- What mysteries can you experience as real and impacting your life if you listen to the words of the *Penitential Rite* and *Kyrie*?
- Can you recognize this as a "mystical experience"?

The Gloria

The Gloria is a very ancient and venerable hymn
in which the Church, gathered together in the Holy Spirit,
glorifies and entreats God the Father and the Lamb.[1]

Glory to God in the highest...
Lord God, heavenly King,
O God, almighty Father.
Lord Jesus Christ, Only Begotten Son...
with the Holy Spirit...

The *Gloria* can be, should be for us, a mystical experience.

It makes us aware of the mystery of our *identification* as a community of people who have heard the Good News. We are empowered by faith to accept it, and by the Spirit to rejoice in it. This is the mystery of grace. To be aware of it is a mystical experience. We need to express it as such.

We are the people who exult to say, *"Glory to God in the highest."* We revel in crying out publicly to God, *"We praise you! We bless you! We adore you! We glorify you!"* Every phrase of the *Gloria* makes us vibrate with awareness. Each excites new gratitude for who God is and what he has done for us. Our enthusiasm proclaims who we are. And who we are should be evident in our enthusiasm.

The *Gloria* is a hymn that was used for morning prayer as early as the fourth century. It gradually became part of the Eucharistic liturgy. At first recited only by the bishop on special days, by the end of the tenth century it was "sung by all the priests and the entire assembly, as we do today." And have been doing for a *thousand years*. Is that already exciting?

This hymn is one of the most beautiful liturgical compositions in existence. It is a genuine treasure for nourishing both personal and communal prayer. A thanksgiving prayer, a "Eucharistic" prayer to God our Creator and our Redeemer, our one unique God in three Persons. It is a veritable *Magnificat* of the Church of the early centuries.[2]

---

[1]*General Instruction on the Roman Missal*, 2002; henceforth *GIRM*, no. 53.
[2]This and much of what follows is translated from *La Messe*, a treasure of a book by Jean-Marie Lustiger, Cardinal Archbishop of Paris, Bayard, 1988.

28

The Cardinal urges us to "meditate at length on every phrase of this splendid act of praise that is the *Gloria*." As an example, he lyricizes about the words that follow: *"Glory to God in the highest, and on earth peace to all whom God loves."*

The phrases accumulate and almost tumble over each other. The words pile up and pull each other along as we express our adoration: *"We praise you, we bless you, we adore you, we glorify you, we give you thanks for your great glory!"* Like an unquenchable spring, exultation and jubilation surge from the depths of our being and spill out of our lips as we contemplate the mystery of God.[3]

One would say the Cardinal is excited by the words of the *Gloria*! We will be excited also, if we think about what we are saying.

The Archbishop, himself of Jewish origin, tells us the *Gloria* puts us into the stance of "all Jewish prayer, which was that of Mary, Zachary, Simeon, of Jesus himself, Saint Paul, all the Apostles." And of the *Eucharistic Prayer* itself. It is *praise and thanksgiving*.

This attitude places us within our relationship to God. It makes us enter into God's action. Our subjectivity, our little personal problems, are swept away in the movement of Love that is God. We learn to love God and so to love other people authentically.

This prayer forms us to a love validated in forgetfulness of self and in giving thanks to God—an action in which we discover our true selves; an action by which the People of God is forged into its call and its mission. A prayer all the more able to bear all the suffering and sins of the world. This is the prayer of Christ that shows us what makes his Eucharist the peak of all prayer.

All of this tells us how important it is for the members of the Church to let themselves be formed to this Eucharistic attitude.

And all of this makes the point again that the *Introductory Rites* impress upon us the *new identity* we have through our unique relationship with God. This is page one of the Good News.

---

[3]*"Peace to all whom God loves"* is the translation quoted by the Cardinal. It is Scripturally and theologically more correct than "to men of good will," because *eudokias* or *bonae voluntatis* (*Luke* 2:14) refers to God's good will toward humans, not vice-versa.

EVANGELIZATION

In summarizing the themes of the early Christian proclamation of the Good News, the *Gloria* is a hymn of *evangelization,* just as the *Creed,* or "Profession of Faith," is an affirmation of *discipleship.* Both are powerful proclamations of Christian belief. But where the *Creed* presents Christian beliefs in the precise words of formulas clarified through study and debate in Church Councils, the *Gloria* simply shouts them from the housetops as Good News. Where the *Creed* is dogmatic, the *Gloria* is kerygmatic.

Although they are equal in depth and intensity, there is a difference in tone between affirming, "We believe in one Lord Jesus Christ, the Only Begotten Son of God, born of the Father before all ages...begotten, not made, consubstantial with the Father" and addressing him directly in a hymn of praise, as "Lord Jesus Christ! Only Begotten Son! Lord God! Lamb of God! Son of the Father!" Both are dramatic declarations, but we feel the difference when we say or sing them. And it should be evident in our tone of voice.

In the "Profession of Faith" we declare what we believe. In the *Gloria* we are ecstatic about it.

In the *Gloria* praise is progressive. We build with increasing intimacy from "Lord God" to "heavenly King," to "God, almighty *Father.*" God is not just the Lord whom we adore. He is the King who has chosen to involve himself in human history; who has drawn close to guide and govern us as his own People. And through Jesus Christ he has accomplished the ultimate closeness: he has become our *Father.*

We *praise* him for what he is; we *bless* him for what he has done. We *adore* him as God, and *glorify* him for his deeds.

All of this accumulates in the cry: *"We give you thanks for your great glory!"*—echoing the beginning of John's Gospel:

> The Word became flesh and made his dwelling among us; and we have seen his glory, the glory of an only Son, coming from the Father, filled with enduring love.

We echo John the Baptizer's first introduction of Jesus: *"Lamb of God, you take away the sins of the world."*[4]

We add, *have mercy on us*, recalling the triple affirmation of *relationship* in the *Kyrie*. Jesus is not just "Lord God." He is the "Lamb of God" who made us one with himself through his blood. He is "Son of the Father," and in him we are "sons and daughters of the Father," *filii in Filio*. Of course we pray, "have mercy on us." We are members of God's family!

Since you "take away the sins of the world, *have mercy on us."* Since you "take away the sins of the world, *receive our prayer."* Since you are "seated at the right hand of the Father—who is also our Father—*have mercy on us."*

These are declarations that say who Jesus is, who we are, and where we stand in relationship to him.

Both the *Gloria* and the *Creed* are bold proclamations of identity. During the *Introductory Rites* we stand for the *Gloria* to identify ourselves as an *evangelized People* rejoicing in the Good News. During the *Liturgy of the Word* we stand again for the *Profession of Faith* to identify ourselves as *disciples* giving unanimous acceptance to the word of God that has just been proclaimed. The *Creed's* focus is on what we believe. The *Gloria's* focus is on what is making us so happy. Both give us something to be excited about. If we *pay attention to the words.* And to why we stand to proclaim them.

"You Alone…"

Modern sensitivity might react against the suggestion of exclusiveness in:

> For you alone are the Holy One; you alone are the Lord; you alone are the Most High, Jesus Christ.

A negative reaction here just means we are not paying attention to the words. We are not saying that Jesus (and by extension his Church) alone is holy. We are saying Jesus alone is *the* Holy One, as we will

---

[4]*John* 1:14; *New American Bible* 1970; *John* 1:29.

say later in the *Creed* that we believe in "one, holy, catholic, and apostolic Church."

People could wrongly interpret both of these statements, as if they said no one who is not consciously and officially a Christian could be holy, and that no figurative representation of the deity venerated by non-Christians could have sacred value. This would rule out the Great Spirit of the Native Americans, everything the Buddha stands for, and any inspiration drawn from the characterizations of the Hindu gods and goddesses, not to mention the values we recognize in Western civilization, artistically symbolized in the "idols" of the Greeks and Romans.

This interpretation put on the *Creed* would open Catholics to the accusation that we see no good in other churches, and do not recognize other Christian denominations as truly "Christian" assemblies. Both interpretations would be unjustified and false.

This is not the place to explain what is true and false in other religions. The bishops assembled for the Second Vatican Council addressed that issue in two documents which come to a head in a Council statement about non-Christian religions: "The Catholic Church rejects nothing of what is true and holy in these religions." So truth and holiness are not limited to explicitly Christian beliefs and practices.[5]

What, then, does it mean to say: *"For you alone are the Holy One, you alone are the Lord, you alone are the Most High, Jesus Christ"*?

In reality it is to proclaim the only valid basis for accepting the truth and goodness found in every religion and world view. The *Gloria* has moved its focus from the Father to the Son. The Jesus we are addressing here is the Second Person of the Trinity, whom John's Gospel calls the "Word," the *Logos*, the intelligibility of God and hence of everything intelligible. When the Father, in creating, says "Let it be!" he gives existence through the "Word" of his knowledge, the Son who is the Truth of all that is:

---

[5]See the *Decree on Ecumenism*, esp. nos. 3, 4 & 6, and the *Declaration on the Relation of the Church to Non-Christian Religions*, esp. nos. 1, 2 and 5.

He is the image of the invisible God, the firstborn of all creation; for in him all things in heaven and on earth were created, things visible and invisible, whether thrones or dominions or rulers or powers—all things have been created through him and for him. He himself is before all things, and in him all things hold together.[6]

As Word, Jesus is the intelligibility of creation. If he were not unique, there could be two different rational explanations of created reality. And whether they were incompatible with each other or just incomplete, there would be no one truth or explanation in which both were rooted. Fundamentally, there would be no unified explanation of the universe.

As it is, since the Word is One, Catholics believe that all worldviews and philosophies—Jewish, Roman, European, African, or Oriental— are united and consistent in whatever truth there is in each one. Saying the *Logos* is One lets us say that all intellectual systems are basically one insofar as they are true. So we are open to the truth in all.

The word "catholic" (*kata-holos*) means "throughout the whole." The One True God of the "catholic" Church is a "catholic" God. Since he is Creator of all, his unique truth and goodness are found "throughout the whole" of all creation, "from the rising of the sun to its setting." We find and respect one Truth and Goodness—that of Jesus Christ, the Word made flesh, the Way, the Truth, and the Life—in whatever is authentically real.[7]

The exclusivity of "You alone..." is also inclusivity. It says Jesus contains, includes in himself all we are looking for. He is not a partial truth, a partial guide to a partial fulfillment. In him alone we have all we need and desire. "We may speak much, and yet shall want words. But the sum of our words is: 'He is All'!"[8]

To proclaim, *"For you alone are the Holy One, you alone are the Lord, you alone are the Most High"* is simply to affirm the One God, the monotheistic God of Jews, Christians, and Muslims alike, who revealed himself to Abraham and Moses, the LORD of the First Commandment: *"Hear, O Israel: The LORD is our God, the LORD alone."*

---

[6]*Colossians* 1:15-17.
[7]*Eucharistic Prayer III.*
[8]If anyone knows where this quote comes from, please tell me.

This is the only God we can love "with *all* our heart, and with *all* our soul, and with *all* our mind, and with *all* our strength." We cannot give our whole selves to a partial good.[9]

If God is not All Truth we cannot love him "with all our mind." If he is not All Good, we cannot love him "with all our heart." The Bread of Life is not one dish offered in a cafeteria line. It is All. This is why Jesus can demand all for All.

John Paul II claims that Jesus gave a "new, specific form" to the First Commandment, and brought it down to an embraceable plan of daily living by re-phrasing it as "Come, follow me." Jesus makes love of the infinite, unimaginable All concrete: "The way and at the same time the content of this [perfect love] consist in the following of Jesus." On ground level. We follow the Word made *flesh*. We keep our feet on the ground, our eyes on Jesus, and we move in a human way toward the "breadth and length and height and depth" of infinite love."[10]

"WITH THE HOLY SPIRIT..."

We end the *Gloria* by bringing things to a conclusion that is also a beginning—as Jesus brought his redemptive mission on earth to its glorious conclusion with the sending of the Holy Spirit at Pentecost, which was the beginning of the mission of the Church.

We add the short phrase. "...*with the Holy Spirit"* to make the Trinitarian structure of the *Gloria* complete—because nothing in Christianity is complete without the inclusion of Father, Son, and Spirit. Whenever God acts "outside of himself," all three Persons act together, although in our human handling of this mystery of "plural unity" we associate the Father, Son, and Spirit with different activities on our behalf.[11]

We say in *Eucharistic Prayer IV* that Jesus "sent the Holy Spirit from you, Father...so that, bringing to perfection his work in the world, he might sanctify creation to the full."

When the Advocate comes, whom I will send to you from the Father, the Spirit of truth who comes from the Father, he will testify on my behalf....

---

[9]See *Deuteronomy* 6:4-5; *Mark* 12:30.
[10]*Ephesians* 3:18. See Benedict's Encyclical *"God is Love,"* December 25, 2005, no. 6; and John Paul II, *The Splendor of Truth,* nos. 18-19.
[11]See the *Catechism of the Catholic Church,* no. 258.

He will guide you into all the truth...and he will declare to you the things that are to come.[12]

The *Gloria* leaves the role of the Holy Spirit open-ended. And leaves us looking forward with expectant hearts to the "more" we will experience, both in the Mass and throughout life.

The *Gloria* ends as it began, with glory: *"...in the glory of God the Father. Amen!!"* This is the glory of God: Father, Son, and Spirit, "three Persons equal in majesty, undivided in splendor, yet one Lord, one God, ever to be adored in your everlasting glory." We end the *Gloria* as we will end every *Eucharistic Prayer*:

Through him, and with him, and in him,
to you, O God, almighty Father,
in the unity of the Holy Spirit,
is all honor and glory,
for ever and ever. Amen.[13]

In praising and thanking God through the *Gloria* we proclaim our identity; we proclaim the Good News; we proclaim the joy we find in both.

QUESTIONS FOR REFLECTION AND DISCUSSION:

- What mysteries can you experience as real and impacting your life if you listen to the words of the *Gloria*?
- What difference would it make if you recited the phrases of the *Gloria* as a conscious act of self-identification?
- What does it mean to say that where the *Creed* is dogmatic, the *Gloria* is "kerygmatic"? What is the goal of each?
- How do you explain that the apparent exclusivity of "You alone..." said of Jesus, is really the basis for respecting the truth and goodness in all religions?
- Why does monotheism require the First Commandment and the First Commandment depend on monotheism?
- If these questions are too abstract, reduce them to one: "What is so great about the *Gloria*?"
- Can you recognize the *Gloria* as a "mystical experience"?

---

[12]*John* 15:36; 16:13. The previous version of the *Eucharistic Prayer* was, "to complete his work on earth and bring us the fullness of grace." The point is not, "Which is better?" but "What nuances of meaning can we find in each?" If we *pay attention to the words!*
[13]See the *Preface* for the Holy Trinity.

The Opening Prayer

The Collect ("Opening Prayer"), the
Prayer over the Offerings, and the Prayer after Communion...
are addressed to God in the name of the entire holy people
and all present, by the priest who presides over the assembly
in the person of Christ.
It is with good reason, therefore, that they are called the
"presidential prayers."
The [presider] invites the people to pray.
All... observe a brief silence so that they may be conscious
that they are in God's presence
and may formulate their petitions mentally.
Then the [presider] says the prayer...
through which the character of the celebration is expressed....
The collect prayer is usually addressed to God the Father,
through Christ, in the Holy Spirit....
The people, uniting themselves to this entreaty, make the prayer
their own with the acclamation "Amen!"[1]

The *Introductory Rites* end with the *"Opening Prayer,"* originally called the "Collect" because it "collected" the prayers of the people.

It is always a Trinitarian prayer, "usually addressed *to* God the Father, *through* Christ the Son *in* [the unity of] the Holy Spirit."[2] It is always the prayer of the whole Church. It is always spoken in the first person plural: "We..."

This is true of the Mass itself. The Mass can never be used as a private devotion. Although "daily celebration is earnestly recommended," ordained priests are forbidden by Canon Law to celebrate Eucharist alone "unless there is a good and reasonable cause for doing so." However, authentic interpretation of the mind of the Church, always kind and nurturing, allows presbyters who experience strong need for or devotion to Eucharist to celebrate alone if they simply cannot find anyone to celebrate with them. The Church points out, however,

---

[1]*GIRM*, nos. 30, 54.
[2]*Ibid.* no. 54. It is good to note that no official, liturgical prayer of the Church is ever addressed to the Virgin Mary or to a Saint. In private, and even public devotions, we pray (the word means "ask") Mary and the Saints to intercede for us. But the Church in her liturgy prays only to God.

that even then it is still "an action of Christ and of the [whole] Church," never the private prayer of the presbyter. The Mass is by nature a *communal* celebration.[3]

As the prayer of the whole Church, the *Opening Prayer* provides a model of what to pray for and how. Archbishop Lustiger writes that the *Opening Prayer* is typically composed of two parts. The first presents, often in a single phrase or under the form of thanksgiving, "some aspect of the mystery of God which the Church proposes that day for our meditation." The second part asks that all present might live out, now and forever, the mystery we are thanking God for.[4]

Examples: the Alternate *Opening Prayer* for:

- *the First Sunday of Advent:*
  Mystery: Father in heaven, our hearts desire the warmth of your love, and our minds are searching for the light of your Word.
  Request: Increase our longing.... give us the strength to grow....

- *the Second Sunday of Advent:*
  Mystery: Father in heaven, the day draws near when the glory of your Son will make radiant the night of the waiting world.
  Request: May the lure of greed not impede us.... May the darkness not blind us....

- *the Third Sunday of Advent:*
  Mystery: Father of our Lord Jesus Christ, ever faithful to your promises and ever close to your Church....
  Request: Prepare our hearts and remove the sadness that hinders us....

---

[3]Canons 904, 908. It distorts our understanding if we ask an ordained priest to offer "your Mass" for an intention. It is not "his" Mass. Canon 901 says, "A priest is entitled to offer Mass for anyone, living or dead." But essentially, every Mass is offered *by Christ and the whole Church for all the intentions for which Jesus offered himself on Calvary.* The Mass does not add to or repeat that sacrifice, but simply makes it *present* on the altar. The presider's intention in offering the Mass has no more value than the intention of any other person present. This statement is not meant to detract from the value of the presider's intention, just to keep it on an equal level with the intentions of the whole assembly. See *Hebrews* 7:22-28; 9:24-28; 10:7-14.
[4]*La Messe*, pp. 85-86. This is verified especially in the "Alternate Opening Prayers" for Sundays.

• *the Fourth Sunday of Advent*:

Mystery: Father, all-powerful God, your eternal Word took flesh on our earth....

Request: Lift our minds in watchful hope to hear the voice....

The Archbishop concludes with the wish that when the presider speaks in the name of all, each one present in the assembly will be deeply conscious and able to say, "It is I who am praying in the name of the Church, and the Church is praying in me."

Does that make it exciting to hear, "Let us pray!"?

QUESTIONS FOR REFLECTION AND DISCUSSION:

• What makes the *"Opening Prayer"*—and all the "presidential prayers"—different from private, devotional prayers?
• In the *"Opening Prayer,"* who is doing the praying?
• Typically, what are the two parts of the *"Opening Prayer"*?
• In the *"Opening Prayer,"* what is the petition based on?

The Liturgy of the Word

The Second Moment of Mystery: Enlightenment by the Living God

"Hallowed be thy name...."

When the Sacred Scriptures are read in the Church,
God himself speaks to his people,
and Christ, present in his own word, proclaims the Gospel.
Therefore, all must listen with reverence to the readings from
God's word, for they make up an
element of greatest importance in the Liturgy....

For in the readings, God speaks to his people,
opening up to them the mystery of salvation...
and Christ himself is present
in the midst of the faithful through his word....

The Liturgy of the Word is to be celebrated in such a way as to
promote meditation, in which...
the word of God may be
grasped by the heart.[1]

The *Liturgy of the Word* should be a mystical experience.

We may think of the *Liturgy of the Word* as a time to sit back, listen to the readings, and hope perhaps to learn something. And, except for the sitting back, it is that. Actually, we should be sitting—mentally, at least—on the edge of the pew, *intent* on learning something. We listen to the readings, not as an "audience," but as *disciples*. The word means "students," not "followers of Jesus." And we are disciples of Jesus Christ only as long as we are students of his, seeking him out to be taught, sitting at his feet, listening to his words and reflecting on them. Jesus described a disciple as someone who "*comes* to me, *hears* my words, and *acts* on them." He gives three characteristics:

---

[1] *General Instruction on the Roman Missal*, 2002 (*GIRM*), nos. 29, 55-56.

1. We *come* to Jesus, *confront* his words, read them or call them into memory. At Mass we *listen*. With attention.

2. We *hear* what he says. Jesus reproached his apostles: "Do you have eyes, and fail to see? Do you have ears, and fail to hear? And do you not remember?" To really "hear" the word of God it is not enough to listen with attention; we have to *reflect* on what we hear. Otherwise the seed of his word falls on "shallow ground," gets a superficial reception, goes in one ear, out the other, and blows away. (How much do you remember of the last reading or homily you heard at Mass? Was it out of your mind before you were even out of the church? "Shallow ground!")

3. We *act* on what we hear. We have to reflect on his words *until* we take a stance toward them. Until we come to *choices*. The seed of God's word does not take root in our lives until it reaches the level of choices.

Other seeds fell on rocky ground, where they did not have much soil, and they sprang up quickly.... But when the sun rose, they were scorched; and since they had no root, they withered away.[2]

So far so good. But there is more:

There is an aspect of the *Liturgy of the Word* that...is deeper than the aspect of instruction.... It is, above all else, a service of communal *prayer*, a celebration of *God speaking to us*.... To be an authentic liturgical event, it has to evoke a sense that God is speaking to us.[3]

That is a mystical experience!

It is, first of all, the experience of *encounter*. In listening to his word, we don't just "come to" Jesus; he comes to us. His "real presence" is in his words. "He is present in his word, since it is he himself who speaks when the holy Scriptures are read in church."

The Church has always venerated the divine Scriptures just as she venerates the body of the Lord, since, especially in the sacred liturgy, she unceas-

---

[2]*Luke 6:47-49; Matthew 13:55-6, 20-21.*
[3]Ralph A. Keifer, *To Give Thanks and Praise*, Pastoral Press, 1980, p. 117. Emphasis added. Pastoral Press is the publication division of the National Association of Pastoral Musicians, "musicians and clergy dedicated to fostering the art of musical liturgy." This puts the weight of informed experience behind their publications.

ingly receives and offers to the faithful the bread of life from the table both of God's word and of Christ's Body....

For in the sacred books, the Father who is in heaven meets his children with great love and speaks with them, and the force and power in the word of God is so great that it stands as the support and energy of the Church, the strength of faith for her sons and daughters, the food of the soul, the pure and everlasting source of spiritual life.[4]

Keifer draws the conclusion:

True celebration of the Word is not simply a matter of putting across what the Lord has said... but first of all communicating a sense that we are privileged and graced and blessed by his very speaking to us.... The point of the *Liturgy of the Word* is not merely to inform people about a message, but to *bring them into communion* with the God whose message is proclaimed.

In other words, a mystical experience of encounter with God.

GETTING DOWN TO PRACTICE

How do we make this mystical experience happen—for ourselves and others?

The basic principle for simply avoiding boredom at Mass is: *Pay attention to the words.* The words are exciting—if we listen, and ask ourselves what they mean.

We should add: *Pay attention to what you see.* The Mass speaks to us through gestures and symbols as well as words.

For example, in the entrance, the Book of the Gospels is carried in, held aloft for all to see, and placed with reverence on the altar. This is to signal the importance of the word of God in the liturgy we are about to celebrate. We should let it move us to interior reverence, expressed in some bodily gesture, if only an inclination of the head. Just as we never enter church without genuflecting to the Blessed Sacrament or bowing to the altar, we should never be consciously in the presence of the word of God without some act of recognition. This puts us in the mode—and mood—of prayer.

We should notice that the book used for the readings is specially bound and beautiful, as is worthy of the word of God. The lector

---

[4]See the documents of Vatican II, *On the Sacred Liturgy*, no. 7; *On Divine Revelation*, no. 21, reprinted at the beginning of the *New American Bible*.

does not read from a throwaway leaflet missal. And before the reading of the Gospel, the *Book of the Gospels* is carried from the altar to the "ambo" or pulpit, accompanied by altar servers with candles. Before reading the Gospel, the deacon "makes the Sign of the Cross on the book and on his forehead, lips, and breast." We can do the same, being aware as we do of what we are expressing.[5]

We should notice that the ambo is used only for the proclamation of the word of God, just as the altar is used only for offering the sacrifice. Songs are led and announcements made from another place, just as vessels for water and washing hands are placed on a side table, not on the altar. This sends a message.

We should let all of this draw us into mystery and prayer. That is what the *Liturgy of the Word* is designed to do. It "is to be celebrated in such a way as to promote *meditation*...avoiding any kind of haste that hinders recollection. It is also appropriate to include brief periods of silence [so that] the word of God may be grasped by the heart and a response prepared through prayer and the prompting of the Holy Spirit." "By *silence and singing* the people *make God's word their own*."[6]

THE RESPONSORIAL PSALM

"By their *singing*...." This explains why the *Responsorial Psalm* is an important moment for facilitating the "mysticism of encounter." Its purpose is not just to provide a break between the readings! It is "an integral part of the *Liturgy of the Word* and holds great liturgical and pastoral importance, because it fosters meditation on the word of

---

[5]The presider should not read any of the readings, including the Gospel, unless no other appropriate minister is available. The *General Instruction on the Roman Missal* is clear. All of the participants at Mass should do "all and only" what their role calls for. "The celebration of the Eucharist is an action of the whole Church, and in it each one should carry out solely but completely that which pertains to him or her" (no. 5). "The function of proclaiming the readings is *ministerial, not presidential*" (no. 59). Knowing this makes us aware that the Mass is a *communal* prayer, not something the ordained priest does and the people just share in. The presider's role is as limited as any other, and it is just as inappropriate for him to add to it by proclaiming the Word of God as it would be for the altar server to distribute the Body of Christ in Communion.
[6]*GIRM*, nos. 55-56.

God.... It is preferable that the *Responsorial Psalm* be sung.... If the Psalm cannot be sung, then it should be recited in such a way that it is particularly suited to fostering meditation on the word of God."

The *Responsorial Psalm* is intended to set the tone for the whole of the *Liturgy of the Word*, to evoke an atmosphere that communicates the tone, mood, and quality of the day's proclamation.... It is a way in which the people take the word of the Lord for the day, make it their own, and proclaim it prayerfully.[7]

If we consciously make the *Responsorial Psalm* our prayerful response to God who has spoken to us in the reading, singing it to him intentionally, as if we were standing face-to-face (which we are!), it will make us more aware of encountering him, the living God, as his words are read to us. "By their *silence and singing* the people *make God's word their own.*"

THE GOSPEL AND SEQUELS

Special solemnity surrounds the reading of the Gospel. We stand, not because the Gospel is more the word of God than the other readings, but because so many of its words are the words of Jesus himself. We stand in recognition of Jesus present and proclaiming his own words in and through the lector. For the same reason we sing the "*Alleluia*" acclamation, "by which the assembly greets the Lord who is about to speak to us in the Gospel and professes its faith by means of the chant." We are rejoicing in Jesus present among us. As the Council declared, "In the liturgy God speaks to his people, Christ is still proclaiming his Gospel." The same Jesus who "went throughout Galilee, teaching in their synagogues and proclaiming the good news of the kingdom" is doing it here and now for us. Encounter with him is a mystical experience.[8]

The reading of the Gospel is the high point of the *Liturgy of the Word*. The Liturgy itself teaches that great reverence is to be shown to it by setting it off from the other readings with special marks of honor; whether on the part of the minister appointed to proclaim it, who prepares himself by a blessing or prayer; or on the part of the faithful, who stand as they listen to it being read and through their acclamation acknowledge and

---

[7]*GIRM*, no. 61, and Keifer, *op. cit.* p. 123.
[8]*GIRM,* no. 62; *Vatican* II *On the Sacred Liturgy*, no. 33. *Matthew* 4:21; 9:35.

confess Christ present and speaking to them; or by the very marks of reverence that are given to the *Book of the Gospels*.[9]

The homily after the Gospel is a presidential function. It "should ordinarily be given by the priest celebrant himself. He may entrust it to a concelebrating priest or occasionally...to the deacon." To show how seriously the liturgy takes the observance of defined roles, the *Instruction* continues: "In *particular cases* and *for a just cause*, the homily *may even* be given by a Bishop...."[10]

The "purpose of the *Profession of Faith*, or *Creed*, is that the whole gathered people may *respond to the word of God* proclaimed in the readings and explained in the homily, and call to mind and confess the *great mysteries of faith*...before these mysteries are celebrated in the Eucharist."[11]

The *Profession of Faith* can be a mystical experience, if we are aware of the mystery in what we are professing. And of the mystery experienced in the fact we can profess it. No one can believe the truths we profess in the *Creed* except by the divine gift of faith, the gift of sharing in God's own knowing act. The gift of knowing what only God can know and as only God can know it. To recite the *Profession of Faith* with *awareness* of this is to experience *enlightenment* by the Holy Spirit.

If we *pay attention to the words* as we say them, reciting the *Profession of Faith* will be for us a mystical experience of the enlightening presence of God in us, empowering us to know and believe the words we pronounce.[12]

The *Prayer of the Faithful* should make us proud to be Catholics. The Church turns outwards in love and concern for others. The *Missal* calls it the *"Universal Prayer"* or *"Prayer of the Faithful."* The words to notice are "universal" and "of the faithful."

By the word "universal" the Church is trying to get us beyond shortsighted concern for our own well-being and that of our limited circle of family and friends. Such concern is good, of course. It is just not the inspiration of the "Universal Prayer," in which "petitions are

---

[9]*GIRM*, 2002, no. 60.
[10]*GIRM*, no. 66.
[11]*Ibid*, no. 67.
[12]*Matthew* 11:27; *Romans* 8:15-16; *Galatians* 4:6; *1Corinthians* 12:3.

offered for the holy Church, for civil authorities, for those weighed down by various needs, for all men and women, and for the salvation of the whole world." Our focus is worldwide. We pray for "the holy Church" and "civil authorities," because both are engaged in fostering the *common good*. We "associate ourselves in prayer with those who are particularly called to serve others... [in] affirmation of our own solidarity in suffering and service with the whole of the human race."

This is not the time or place to pray for our individual intentions, to ask for special graces to meet particular challenges we are facing in our life. Petitions that begin with, "That we may...." are good petitions in themselves, but they are missing the point unless they conclude with something like "...come to the aid of *all those* afflicted by...." The *Universal Prayer* is not a prayer in which this particular congregation, or the Church as a whole, prays for its own needs, although in the *Instruction*, prayer "for the local community" is not excluded. It is a prayer that *turns outwards* in love and concern for the whole human race. It is a "catholic" prayer that makes one proud to be a Catholic.

It is also called the prayer *"of the faithful"* because it is a prayer in which "the people...exercising the office of their *baptismal priest-hood*, offer prayers to God for the salvation of all." It is:

the prayer through which *the laity especially* express their ministry of prayer for the needs of the human race. Participation in this prayer was seen as a special privilege of the baptized.... Catechumens [only] joined in this prayer at the Easter Vigil when they were baptized and shared in the Eucharist for the first time.

This explains why the *Instruction* "purposely does not list the ordained priest as one of those whom it is desirable to have lead the prayer...."

Since the prayer is supposed to be an expression of concern for the needs of the human race, it is highly desirable that the minister who announces these intentions be a person who has obvious ministry to human need—a deacon, a sister who cares for the sick, a layperson who has such a ministry visible to the community.

The *Prayer of the Faithful* is, first and foremost, intended to be a manifestation of the people's ministry. If the ordained priest declares the intentions, the prayer becomes experienced as one more celebrant's prayer to which the people only assent. Conversely, if one who has a concrete and known ministry to the needy stands before the congregation to lead them in prayer for the helpless of the world, the prayer cannot help but have a new urgency and sense of reality.

We should note that in the *Prayer of the Faithful*, "it is the people who do the actual praying." The rest—"the presider's introduction, the statements of intentions—are not prayers at all. They are invitations to pray."[13]

The *Liturgy of the Word* is a mystical experience of *encounter* with God and *enlightenment* through the proclamation of his word.

Does that, or does that not, make the Mass exciting?

QUESTIONS FOR DISCUSSION

- How can I guarantee I will never be bored at Mass?
- What mystical experiences should we be having during the *Liturgy of the Word*?
- What can we do during the *Liturgy of the Word* to be conscious of these mystical experiences?

KEY POINTS: WHAT CAN I SAY NOW ABOUT:

The *Responsorial Psalm.*
The reading of the Gospel?
The *Profession of Faith*?
The *Prayer of the Faithful*?

---

[13]For these (slightly edited) quotes and other ideas above, see Keifer, *op. cit.* pp.127-131. See also *GIRM*, no. 69.

The Presentation of Gifts

The Third Moment of Mystery:
Empowerment by the Holy Spirit

"Thy Kingdom come...."

At the beginning of the Liturgy of the Eucharist, the gifts, which will become Christ's Body and Blood, are brought to the altar.

It is desirable that the participation of the faithful be expressed by members of the congregation bringing up the bread and wine for the celebration of the Eucharist.

Sufficient hosts and wine for the communion of the faithful are to be prepared. It is most important that the faithful should receive the body of the Lord in hosts consecrated at the same Mass and should share the cup.... Communion is thus a clearer sign of sharing in the sacrifice which is actually taking place.[1]

The [presider] may incense the gifts placed upon the altar... so as to signify the Church's offering and prayer rising like incense in the sight of God.[2]

The *Presentation of Gifts* can be a lost moment in the Mass. If the gifts are not brought up in a solemn procession, passing through the whole assembly, to be placed in the hands of the presider, the putting of the chalice, bread, and wine on the altar can be just a "housekeeping" moment—like changing the props between scenes during a play. To reduce the *Presentation of Gifts* to this would be to lose a precious movement in the celebration of Eucharist.

The *Presentation of Gifts* is a summons to be aware of the mystery of being *called by God.* To be aware of it through the act of consciously *responding.*

---

[1]These two paragraphs are from the directions in the 1985 *Sacramentary.* They are not as complete in the new *Roman Missal* but the teaching and intention are the same.

[2]*General Instruction on the Roman Missal*, 2002; (*GIRM*), nos. 73-75.

To be aware of this mystery as real and impacting my life right now is to have a mystical experience. To enter into this, I need to pay attention to what I hear and see; to ask what the words and actions mean.

First there is the significance of the procession itself. The 1985 *Sacramentary* says clearly *"it is desirable"* that the bread and wine be brought up *"by members of the congregation"* because this expresses *"the participation of the faithful"* in the celebration of the Eucharist. The primary thrust and repeated intention of the Vatican Council's reform of the liturgy was to restore and encourage the visible, active participation of the laity in the Eucharistic celebration that had been taken away from them over the course of previous centuries. This is the expressed intention and desire of the bishops who speak for the Catholic Church:

> It is very much the wish of the Church that all the faithful should be led to take that *full, conscious, and active part* in liturgical celebrations which is demanded by the very nature of the liturgy, and to which the Christian people, "a chosen race, a royal priesthood, a redeemed people" *have a right* and *to which they are committed* by reason of their Baptism.[3]

This is also the reason why there should be as many hosts on the paten (plate) that is brought up in the procession as there are people present at Mass:

> It is most important that the faithful should receive the body of the Lord in hosts consecrated at the same Mass and should share the cup when it is permitted. Communion is thus *a clearer sign of sharing in the sacrifice which is actually taking place.*

In the procession every person present in the pews is symbolically being brought forward, represented by a host on the paten, to be placed on the altar. That is why the gifts are brought up from the back, passing through the whole congregation. It is to say the whole assembly is coming forward, "presenting their bodies as a living

---

[3]Vatican II, *Sacred Liturgy.* nos. 11, 14. For those unfamiliar with the laity's exclusion from full, active participation in the Mass, Bishop Patrick Dunn of Auckland, New Zealand, explains it succinctly in his book *Priesthood: A Re-Examination of the Roman Catholic Theology of the Presbyterate*: Alba House, New York, 1990, pages 81-85. See also Bernard Botte, O.S.B., *From Silence to Participation: An Insider's View of Liturgical Renewal,* translated by John Sullivan, O.C.D., The Pastoral Press, 225 Sheridan St. NW, Washington D.C. 20011, 1988.

sacrifice," as they did on the day of their Baptism, to be placed on the altar and offered with Jesus during the *Eucharistic Prayer* as one with him in the mystery of his sacrifice on the cross.[4]

This is a reaffirmation of Baptism. It is the "Catholic altar call." By placing ourselves on the altar with the bread and wine we are saying, as adults, that we *accept and embrace* our *Baptism*; that we *understand and are entering into* what is being done and expressed at *Mass*; that we want to be part of it.

We are also pledging ourselves to *continual conversion*; that is, to making *constant changes* in our lifestyle.

The bread and wine are being put on the altar to be transformed. We put ourselves on the altar with them to be transformed—not into the body and blood of Christ, since we already are that by Baptism— but into the "perfect image" of Christ that Baptism committed us to grow into. This is a pledge of continual conversion which, as we shall see, is a renewal of our baptismal consecration to bear *witness* to the Gospel by a lifestyle unintelligible without it.

The prayer the presider says as he holds up the gifts is almost identical for the bread and wine:

Blessed are you, Lord God of all creation,
for through your goodness we have received
the bread (wine) we offer you:
fruit of the earth (vine) and work of human hands,
it will become for us the bread of life (our spiritual drink).

This is a very theological prayer. It summarizes the mystery of redemption, the mystery of grace, by which what is created has become divine.

Like the bread and wine, which represent us, we are the "fruit of the earth"—of generation from our parents' bodies. And like the gifts, transformed by the "*work of human hands*" from wheat and grapes into bread and wine, we too are the "work of human hands." What we are at this moment, as we present ourselves to God, is the fruit, the "work" of all the *choices* we have made throughout our lives; the choices that have formed us into the persons we are.

---

[4]See *Romans* 12:1-2. This is the "theme text" for the *Presentation of Gifts*.

49

God created our human natures. "What" we are by our nature is the same in all of us. But we create ourselves as persons. "Who" we are as persons is unique in each one of us. What our "name" means at any given moment is the cumulative effect of all the free responses we have made to life, to others, to God, since we were born. What we hold up to God in the *Presentation of Gifts* is our present selves: *"fruit of the earth and work of human hands."*

In every Mass we recommit to the mystery of our Baptism. We do it with the increased understanding we have grown into (even since the previous day or week) of what our baptismal commitment involves. Of what it asks and what it promises.

We do this, however, conscious of the *mystery* of redemption. The bread *"will become for us the bread of life."* And the wine will become *"our spiritual drink."* What "earth has given" is going to be made divine. In the same way, by the transforming miracle of our incorporation into Christ at Baptism, we, though human, are to be communicators of the "bread of life" to others. We are to give others "spiritual drink." We have "become Christ." We have been made divine. We "present our bodies as a living sacrifice to God" so that Christ might *use them* as the medium of his own self-expression. *With us, in us, and through us,* Jesus Christ will express—in the flesh, through our physical words and actions—the divine truth we know through the gift of faith; the divine promise we live for by the gift of hope; the divine love we give to God and others as the gift of his own love poured out in our hearts. Our daily expression of this is animated at Mass:

With love we celebrate his death.
With living faith we proclaim his resurrection.
With unwavering hope we await his return in glory.[5]

We are *called*, we are *empowered*, we are *sent*, to bear witness to Jesus Christ by *living on the level of God*. This is Pope Paul VI's definition of Christian *witness*:

Anyone who rereads in the New Testament the origins of the Church, follows her history step by step and watches her live and act, sees that she is linked to *evangelization* in her most intimate being:

---

[5]Weekday *Preface* V.

...The Church remains in the world when the Lord of glory returns to the Father. She remains as a sign—simultaneously obscure and luminous—of a new presence of Jesus, of his departure and of his permanent presence. She prolongs and continues him.

And it is above all his mission and his condition of being an evangelizer that she is called upon to continue. For the Christian community is never closed in upon itself.... This intimate life only acquires its full meaning when it becomes a *witness*, when it evokes admiration and conversion, and when it becomes the preaching and proclamation of the Good News. Thus it is the whole Church that receives the mission to evangelize, and the work of each individual member is important for the whole.

The Church is an evangelizer, but she begins by being evangelized herself.

By putting ourselves on the altar in the *Presentation of Gifts* we commit ourselves to the "new evangelization"—to embodying the Good News ever more visibly in our own lives and through our lifestyle proclaiming it to others. But what we need to embody is not just good human virtue; it is the divine life of God in us; the presence of the risen, living Jesus in us; a way of acting and living that can only be explained by the Gift of the Holy Spirit.

Above all the Gospel must be proclaimed by *witness*. Take a Christian or a handful of Christians who, in the midst of their own community...radiate in an altogether simple and unaffected way their faith in *values that go beyond current values*, and their *hope in something that is not seen* and that one would not dare to imagine. Through this wordless witness these Christians *stir up irresistible questions* in the hearts of those who see how they live: Why are they like this? Why do they live in this way? What or who is it that inspires them? Why are they in our midst? Such a witness is already a silent proclamation of the Good News....

All Christians are called to this *witness*, and in this way they can be real evangelizers.

The key phrase here is "stir up irresistible questions." To bear witness, to be authentically Christian, our lifestyle has to *raise eyebrows*. If it can be understood without specific reference to the values taught by Jesus Christ, it is not specifically Christian and does not bear witness to the Gospel.

For the Church, evangelizing means bringing the Good News into all the strata of humanity, and through its influence transforming humanity from within and making it new: "Now I am making the whole of creation new."

51

But there is no new humanity if there are not first of all *new persons renewed by Baptism* and by *lives lived according to the Gospel.*[6]

To put ourselves on the altar with the bread and wine during the *Presentation of Gifts* is to commit ourselves—consciously, freely, deliberately, as adults—to the *mission* of bearing witness to the Good News of Jesus Christ. This is simply to reaffirm and accept our baptismal consecration as *prophets*.

Prophets are those who "profess" the faith, not in words only, but through a lifestyle that does not make sense without it. This is our first acceptance of, our first response to, the *mission* of Jesus, which is the mission of the Church.

We become adults, mature Christians in the Church, on the day we embrace the Church's mission as our own. Until then, St. Paul says we are not "spiritual people, but rather...people of the flesh... infants in Christ" to be fed "with milk, not solid food," because we are "not ready for solid food." As long as we are in the Church, or participating in Eucharist, just for "what we get out of it," we are still children. Children are not expected to work. They are committed only to growing and developing so they will be able to work and contribute something to the human race when they grow up. Paul's teaching is that we are not "grown-up" Christians until we are committed to "building up the Church." He says, "When I was a child, I spoke like a child, I thought like a child, I reasoned like a child; but when I became an adult, I put an end to childish ways." In every Mass the *Presentation of Gifts* invites us to "build up the Church," and through the Church the world.

> To each is given the manifestation of the Spirit for the common good.... So since you are eager for spiritual gifts, strive to excel in them for building up the church.... When you come together... let all things be done for building up.

This is an important step in letting Christ grow to "full stature" in us:

> The gifts he gave were... to *equip the saints for the work* of ministry, for *building up the body of Christ*, until all of us come to the unity of the faith and of the knowledge of the Son of God, to maturity, to the measure of the full stature of Christ.

---

[6]*Evangelization in the Modern World*, nos. 15, 18, 21.

All the gifts we have received from God, all that we return to him by placing ourselves on the altar in the *Presentation of Gifts*, are gifts given to us for "building up the Church." This is what we ask for in the *Prayer over the Gifts*:

> Lord, accept our sacrifice as a holy exchange of gifts. By offering what you have given us, may we receive the gift of yourself.[7]

RESPONSIBLE OBEDIENCE

It is important that everyone know what is being expressed in this movement of the Mass. The bishops insisted in the Second Vatican Council:

> In order that the liturgy may be able to produce its full effects, it is necessary that the faithful come to it with proper dispositions, that their minds be attuned to their voices.... Pastors of souls must, therefore, realize that, when the liturgy is celebrated, their obligation *goes further than simply ensuring that the laws* governing valid and lawful celebration are observed. They must *also ensure that the faithful take part fully aware* of what they are doing, actively engaged in the rite and enriched by it....

Consistent with this, the *General Instruction on the Roman Missal* prescribes:

> It is also up to the priest, in the exercise of his office of presiding over the gathered assembly, to *offer certain explanations* that are foreseen in the rite itself. Where it is indicated in the rubrics, the celebrant is *permitted to adapt them* somewhat in order that they respond to the understanding of those participating. However, he should always take care to keep to the sense of the text given in the Missal and to express them succinctly.[8]

A good example of a prayer the presider is "permitted to adapt"— and perhaps even required to adapt in the spirit of the *Instruction's* mandated goal of making the liturgy "respond to the understanding of those participating"—is the prayer said while "the deacon, or the [presider] pours wine and a little water into the chalice, saying quietly: *'By the mystery of this water and wine may we come to share in the divinity of Christ who humbled himself to share in our humanity.'*"

---

[7]*1Corinthians* 3:1-2 and Paul's "hymn to maturity": chapters 12 through 14; *Ephesians* 4:11-13; cf. Twentieth Sunday in Ordinary Time.
[8]Vatican II on the *Sacred Liturgy*. nos. 11, 14; *General Instruction on the Roman Missal*, 2002, no. 31.

It would follow, from the spirit of the Council and *Instruction* texts quoted, that the presider should 1. speak these words loudly enough to be heard; and 2. make any changes in them necessary for their meaning to be understood.

The new *Roman Missal* directs that the presider should say this prayer, as well as the ones beginning, *"Blessed are you, Lord God of all creation..."* in a "low voice" or "quietly." The *1985 Sacramentary* says, "inaudibly." We need to interpret this, however, in the light of the *General Instruction* statement that "The procession bringing the gifts is accompanied by the Offertory chant which *continues at least until* the gifts have been placed on the altar." Combine this with the *Roman Missal*'s instruction that "If the Offertory Chant is not sung, the priest may speak these words aloud; and at the end, the people may acclaim: *'Blessed be God for ever.'"* The point seems to be that if there is singing that would make the words inaudible anyway, the presider should speak them in a low voice. But if there is no singing, or if it stops when the gifts are placed on the altar (which seems to be the *Instruction*'s preference), then he should proclaim them to the assembly so that they might make the words their own in an acclamation.

We need to see this in the light of the *General Instruction* explanation that:

> The nature of the "presidential" texts demands that they be spoken in a loud and clear voice and that everyone listen with attention. Thus, while the priest is speaking these texts, there should be no other prayers or singing, and the organ or other musical instruments should be silent.

This is because "The priest... as the one who presides, prays in the name of the Church and of the assembled community." There are a few times in the Mass, however, when "he prays only in his own name, asking that he may exercise his ministry with greater attention and devotion." Those prayers are said "in a low voice," and the prayers at the *Presentation of Gifts* are specifically mentioned here.

There is an ambiguity, however, because the prayers at the *Presentation of Gifts* are clearly not just "asking that the presider may exercise his ministry with greater attention and devotion." Two of them provide for a response from the assembly, and the other asks: "By the mystery of this water and wine *may we come to share...*," which includes the assembly. It would seem obvious that if we read the liturgical instructions with the intelligence the Church expects of us, the Church's preference is for whatever favors "full, conscious, active participation" by the assembly. Vatican II makes it the presider's duty to "*ensure that the faithful take part fully aware* of what they are doing, actively engaged in the rite and enriched by it."[9]

To obey this command, we need to "adapt to the understanding of those participating" the wording of the prayer: "*By the mystery of this water and wine may we come to share in the divinity of Christ who humbled himself to share in our humanity.*" The meaning is not fully and immediately obvious. If the presider knows that not everyone is aware of the tradition that sees the wine as representing Christ or his divinity, and the water as representing us or his humanity, he needs to act to "*ensure that the faithful take part fully aware* of what they are doing."

What the words, with their accompanying gesture, are saying is:

May what we express by the mingling of this water and wine
bring us more deeply into the mystery
of being poured out in Baptism
to be lost and found in the divinity of Christ,
as he was poured out in his Incarnation
to be lost and found in our humanity.

Through these or equivalent words, the presider should "ensure" that all in the assembly are conscious of the basic mystery being expressed here: the mystery of our redemption; the mystery of the created and the Uncreated, the human and the divine being made one "in Christ." This is the "mystery of the Father's will, according to his good pleasure that he set forth in Christ, as a plan for the fullness of time, *to gather up all things in him, things in heaven and things on earth.*" Henceforth it is not enough to be merely human. To be authentically Christian, all we are and do must be, as much as possible, "fully human and fully divine."

We offer ourselves consciously to this transformation in the *Presentation of Gifts*. We pledge to keep trying to match our behavior to this ideal, so that our lifestyle will bear witness to the Good News

---

[9]*GIRM*, nos.32-33. Vatican II, *Sacred Liturgy*. nos. 11, 14.

of Jesus Christ. We pledge to be *witnesses* and *evangelizers*. To "be Church."

The presider invites all present to make the sacrifice their own: "Pray, brothers and sisters, that my sacrifice and yours may be acceptable to God, the almighty Father."

The people then "rise and reply":

May the Lord accept the sacrifice at your hands
for the praise and glory of his name,
for our good
and the good of all his holy Church.

This is to make one's own all that the sacrifice expresses and intends. This is the "mystical experience" of the *Presentation of Gifts*.

QUESTIONS FOR REFLECTION AND DISCUSSION:

- What does the *Presentation of Gifts* invite us to do?
- Why are the gifts brought forward from the back of the Church?
- Why should there be the same number of hosts on the plate as there are people present at Mass?
- What makes the *Presentation of Gifts* like a Baptist "altar call"?
- Why is the *Presentation of Gifts* a pledge of "continual conversion"?
- What does the prayer the presider says as he holds up the gifts teach us about the nature of Christian *witness*?
- What fundamental Christian mystery does the mingling of the water and wine remind us of?
- How does the *Presentation of Gifts* make us aware of the mystery of *call* as real and impacting our consciousness right now? How is our response to this a mystical experience?

KEY POINTS: WHAT CAN I SAY NOW ABOUT:

Making the *Presentation of Gifts* a deep, personal act?

The *Procession* to bring up the gifts?

The theology expressed in the prayer the presider says as he holds up the gifts?

The assembly's response to the invitation, "Pray, brothers and sisters, that my sacrifice and yours may be acceptable to God, the almighty Father"?

The Eucharistic Prayer

The Fourth Moment of Mystery: Surrender and Union in Ministry

"Thy will be done"

Now the center and summit of the entire celebration begins:
namely, the Eucharistic Prayer...

In the Eucharistic Prayer, thanks is given to God for the whole
work of salvation, and the offerings become
the Body and Blood of Christ.

The chief elements making up the Eucharistic Prayer are:
a. Thanksgiving; b. Acclamation; c. Epiclesis; d. Institution
narrative and consecration; e. Anamnesis; f. Offering;
g. Intercession; h. Final doxology.

The Church's intention is that the faithful
not only offer this spotless Victim but also
learn to offer themselves,
and so day by day to be consummated, through Christ the
Mediator, into unity
with God and with each other,
so that at last God may be all in all.[1]

The *Eucharistic Prayer* is a mystery—and unfortunately, it is a mystery barely understood by most Catholics.

In itself, the *Eucharistic Prayer* is the mystery at the heart of the Mass. A "mystery" is defined, not as "something that cannot be understood," but as "a truth that invites *endless exploration.*"

"Endless" because a mystery always deals with the truth of God, who is "infinite," which means "without limits." God is endless Truth, inexhaustible Goodness, unlimited Being.

---

[1] *General Instruction on the Roman Missal, (GIRM),* nos. 2, 72, 78, 79, 30.

A mystical *experience* is a moment of conscious interaction with God. In urging that "all the faithful should be led to take their *full, conscious, and active part*" in the Eucharistic celebration, the bishops of the Second Vatican Council were hoping to make the Mass a mystical experience for everyone present.[2]

The key to entering into the mystical experience of the *Eucharistic Prayer* is very simple. All we have to do is understand what is happening and consciously enter into it.

What is happening is that Jesus is making himself present on the altar, not just as "being there," but *in the act* of offering himself on the cross. The sacrifice of Calvary, which took place once and for all two thousand years ago and can never be repeated, is *made present* now in our time and space.

Or we are made present to another time and space. Whether we say Calvary is here or we are there, the point is that *we are present* as Jesus is offering himself on the cross. We are present, and we can participate in it. We are present *in order to be part of the action*.[3]

On the cross, Jesus as Priest offered himself as Victim. At Mass we, who became "priests in the Priest" by Baptism, are also offering him. And as "victims in the Victim" we are also offering ourselves—with him, in him, and through him—as members of his body. Members of the body of Jesus-Priest offering himself. Members of the body of Jesus-Victim being offered for the life of the world.

In the Mass, through Christ and with Christ and in Christ we offer our bodies, our "flesh for the life of the world."[4]

That is a mystical experience. But what does it mean?

---

[2]Vatican II, Sacred Liturgy. nos. 11, 14.

[3]Jesus is also present as rising and as reigning after his return. But our first focus is on Calvary. The Mass is a "remembering" that makes actually present what is remembered. The liturgical word for this is anamnesis, a word that "is practically untranslatable in English. 'Memorial,' 'commemoration,' 'remembrance' all suggest a recollection of the past, whereas anamnesis means making present an object or person from the past." Frank Senn, "Anamnesis," in New Dictionary of Sacramental Worship, ed. Peter Fink, S.J., Liturgical Press 1990. See also John B. Ryan, "Eucharistic Prayers," and Peter Fink, "Eucharist, Theology of..." op. cit.

[4]See *John* 6:51.

Priests and Victims in Action

We aren't physically dying for others. But in a sense we are. The Mass is a celebration of our Baptism, because at Baptism we entered into the mystery being celebrated at Mass. At Baptism we "died in Christ."

Do you not know that all of us who have been baptized into Christ Jesus were baptized into his death? Therefore we have been buried with him by baptism into death, so that, just as Christ was raised from the dead by the glory of the Father, so we too might walk in newness of life.[5]

What we accepted at Baptism was to be incorporated into the body of Christ hanging on the cross. We accepted to die in him, and to rise with him in order to live now, not as ordinary human beings born of our mothers and fathers, but as the body of Christ, reborn as sons and daughters of the Father. We accepted to "die" to this world. We did this in a real way: not just by taking with our wills an emancipated stance toward everything on earth, but by actually giving up our lives, truly dying—not physically, but mystically, in a way more real than physical death—with Christ and in Christ when he died on the cross.

In the eyes of God, the Giver of existence, whose eyes not only see truth but make truth what it is, we gave up our human lives with Jesus on the cross. We were made one with Jesus who said, "I lay down my life in order to take it up again." We gave up our human lives in order to take them up again as both human and divine. We died in Christ to rise with Christ as a "new creation."

This is what Paul meant when he said, "The world has been crucified to me, and I to the world." And, "We know that our old self was crucified with him so that the body of sin might be destroyed, and we might no longer be enslaved to sin." Paul is not talking here about pain, but about two things: a *radical new stance of our wills* toward everything created, and the *mystery of a real dying and rising* in the death and resurrection of Jesus. Both became ours, and we accepted both, on the day of our Baptism. We celebrate both as "the grace of our Lord Jesus Christ" in every Mass.[6]

---

[5]*Romans* 6:3-11.
[6]*John* 10:17; *2Corinthians* 5:14-21; *Galatians* 6:14; *Romans* 6:6.

61

Translated into practical terms for everyday living, what is this "radical new stance" toward everything created that we took at Baptism and reaffirm in the *Eucharistic Prayer* at every Mass?

In one word, it is love.

LIVING IS LOVING IS MINISTRY

"Grace" is defined as "the gift of sharing in the divine life of God." But the life of God is love. To live as God, then, is to love as God.

By Baptism we committed ourselves to love like God. More precisely, we surrendered ourselves to let Jesus Christ love *with us, in us, and through us;* and *express* that love in and through our physical, human words and actions.

This is the essence—and the mystery—of Christian *ministry*.

To live as Christ is to live in love. Divine love. This is the "new commandment" Jesus gave to all who would be his body on earth. He changed the "second greatest" Commandment from "You shall love your neighbor as yourself" to "Love one another *as I have loved you*."

> I give you a new commandment, that you love one another. Just as I have loved you, you also should love one another.... This is my commandment, that you love one another as I have loved you.[7]

Jesus set the example by loving us as the Father loved him: "As the Father has loved me, so I have loved you; abide in my love."

> The Father loved Jesus by giving him the power to give life:
>
> For just as the Father has life in himself, so he has granted the Son also to have life in himself... Indeed, just as the Father raises the dead and gives them life, so also the Son gives life to whomever he wishes....
>
> My Father is still working, and I also am working.... *Very truly, I tell you*, the Son can do nothing on his own, but only what he sees the Father doing; for *whatever the Father does*, the Son does likewise. The Father loves the Son and shows him all that he himself is doing; and he will show him *greater works than these*, so that you will be astonished.

Jesus loves us by giving us the power to give life, as his instruments. He calls us to let him live in us and express himself through us.

---

[7]*John* 13:34; 15:12.

Very truly, I tell you, the one who believes in me will also do the *works that I do* and, in fact, will do *greater works than these*, because I am going to the Father.

You did not choose me but I chose you. And I appointed you to *go and bear fruit, fruit that will last*, so that the Father will give you whatever you ask him in my name.

"Fruit that will last" is eternal life. Jesus gave us the mission he defined as his own: "I came that they may *have life*, and have it *to the full.*"

At Baptism we accepted to live "no longer for ourselves but for him" who came to earth to *give life*. So to live and love as Jesus is to dedicate ourselves to giving and enhancing life, divine life, in others. To nurture. To heal. To help to grow. This is ministry.[8]

Ministry is dying to ourselves in order to live for others in love. To live for others in love is to give life to others. Through ministry—by "presenting our bodies as a living sacrifice to God," so that wherever our live bodies are, Jesus Christ can *express himself* in and through our physical human actions to communicate his divine life to others.

Jesus said, "No one has greater love than this, to lay down one's life for one's friends." And John said this is our call: "We know love by this; that he laid down his life for us—and we ought to lay down our lives for one another."

In practice, we "lay down our lives" for others through *ministry*. Every hour, every minute we give to another in service is an hour or minute of our *life*, because on this earth "life" and "time" are synonymous. And every time we give *expression* to our faith, our hope, our love in bodily words and actions we are "dying to self" because we are making ourselves *vulnerable*. Dying to our fears and reserves. Exposing ourselves. Exposing our personal thoughts and desires.

St. Augustine defined love as wanting another to *esse et bene esse*: to "be and to become all one can be." When we try to help this happen, we are loving in action.

St. Paul described his ministry as bringing Christ to birth and to "full stature" in all those he dealt with. He addresses the Galatians as,

---

[8]*John* 5:17-26; 10:10; 14:12; 15:7-17. See *Eucharistic Prayer IV*.

"My little children, for whom I am again in the *pain of childbirth until Christ is formed* in you...." And he said God gives his gifts to Christians "to equip the saints for the work of *ministry,* for *building up the body of Christ,* until all of us come...to *maturity,* to the measure of the *full stature of Christ.*"[9]

To minister is to respond to others' needs. That is how we know we love. That is how we know we are alive:

> We know that we have passed from death to life because we love one another....We know love by this, that he laid down his life for us—and we ought to lay down our lives for one another. How does God's love abide in anyone who sees a brother or sister in need and yet refuses help? Little children, let us love, not in word or speech, but in truth and action.
>
> God's love was revealed among us in this way: God sent his only Son into the world so that we *might live* through him.... Beloved, since God loved us so much, we also ought to love one another.[10]

No one has greater need than this, to die in Christ in order to live forever. How does God's love abide in us, if we see a brother or sister in this need and yet refuse to help? Everyone's need is for *life.* We live to help all have life "to the full."

"MY BODY, GIVEN UP"

All this is brought into one focal point during the "first elevation" of the *Eucharistic Prayer.* After repeating the words of Jesus, "This is my body... my blood... given up for you," the presider holds up first the host, then the chalice for the assembly to see.

At that moment we have been taught to echo the words Thomas spoke when he saw Jesus after the resurrection: "My Lord and my God!"

These are words of adoration. True words. Appropriate words. But not the words we should say.

It is not that we do not adore Jesus or should not adore his "body and blood, soul and divinity" present in the host, the Blessed Sacra-

---

[9] *Romans* 12:1; *John* 15:13; *1John* 3:16; *Galatians* 4:19; *Ephesians* 4:11-13.
[10] *1John* 3:14-18; 4:7-11.

ment. Of course we adore him. What is held up before our eyes is the Body and Blood of Christ, God himself.

It is just not the time to *focus* on adoration. Our focus should be on the *action* that is taking place. What we are called to do at this moment, what the Church and the liturgy invite us to do, is not simply to be lost in rapt and silent adoration. What we need to do at this moment, must do at this moment if we are going to enter into the mystical experience of "*full, conscious, and active participation*" in the Eucharist, is *join in the action*. This is the moment to offer Jesus as "priests in the Priest," and to offer ourselves as "victims in the Victim" in union with Jesus offering himself on Calvary and in the Mass.

The words we should echo at this moment, proclaiming them in the silent depth of our hearts to God and to every member of the human race, are: "This is *my* body, given up for *you*."

Husbands and wives saying to each other, "This is my body, given up for you." Every member of the congregation saying to every other, "This is my body, given up for you." All of us, in union with Jesus offering himself on the cross, saying to every member of the human race, "This is my body, given up for you."

To family and strangers, friends and enemies; and yes, to all the murderers, rapists, and suicide bombers on the face of the earth, "*This is my body, given up for you*."

This is what it means to take the "*full, conscious, and active part*" in the Eucharistic celebration that the bishops of the Second Vatican Council called for. This is what it means to be authentically at Mass.

This, and only this, is to share personally, fully and authentically in the act of love Jesus made and expressed on the cross. If we do not "offer our bodies" with him for the "life of the world," we simply are not participating in the mystery of the Eucharist.

But if we do...

If we do, we are entering into the mystical experience of loving as Christ loves us.

This is the experience that will take place again, whether we are fully conscious of it or not, every time we "give our bodies" to another in physical acts of ministry. Every time we give physical, bodily expression to our faith, our hope, our love, to enhance the lives of others.

When we give visible expression to the invisible life of God within us, God can use that to communicate divine life to others. Through the audible expression of our faith God can communicate his divine truth. Through the visible, tangible expression of our love God can communicate his divine love. Through our healing, nurturing care for others God can give healing. Give hope. Give life.

This is Christian ministry. This is what we were consecrated to do by the words of our baptismal anointing: *"As Christ was anointed Priest... so live as a member of his body."*

This is the summit of the *Eucharistic Prayer.*

The *General Instruction on the Roman Missal* lists eight "chief elements" that make up the Eucharistic Prayer. They are: *Thanksgiving, Acclamation, Epiclesis, Institution Narrative* (or Consecration), *Anamnesis, Offering, Intercession, Final Doxology.* We will take up each of these in the *Reflections* that follow.

Questions for Reflection and Discussion:

- What mystery does the *Eucharistic Prayer* make real as present and impacting my life right now?
- Is this a "mystical experience"?
- How is this mystery involved in both the Mass and Baptism?
- What are the best words to say in our hearts during the "first elevation"?
- In terms of daily life, how do we "offer our bodies for the life of the world"?

Key Points: What can I say now about:

The *Eucharistic Prayer*?

Our baptismal consecration as *priests*?

The *Institution Narrative*?

Christ's promise, "I chose you… to *go and bear fruit, fruit that will last*"?

The Rite of Communion

The Fifth Moment of Mystery: A Preview of Victory

"Give us... Forgive us"

> *Since the Eucharistic Celebration is the Paschal Banquet,*
> *it is desirable that in keeping with the Lord's command,*
> *his Body and Blood should be received*
> *as spiritual food by the faithful who are properly disposed.*[1]

The *Rite of Communion* is an anticipation of the "end time." We celebrate Christ's victory, the triumph of his coming in glory at the end of time to "gather up all things in Christ." It is a preview of the "wedding banquet of the Lamb." A foretaste of heaven.[2]

The "end time" is our focus, and our all-absorbing desire. We long for, dream of, strive and work for the realization of the "mystery of God's will," that he "set forth in Christ, as a plan for the fullness of time." That is to *"bring all things in the heavens and on earth into one under Christ's headship."* Communion is a preview of this that gives courage and motivates us, as *stewards* of the kingship of Christ, to abandon to God all we have and are, to manage and use everything under our control only to accomplish God's plan, *to transform society* by bringing every area and activity of human life on earth under his life-giving rule.[3]

In the "eternal now" of God's time, Christ's victory is already an accomplished fact. But in our earthly time it is still to be brought to completion. This is our task. This is the meaning of our baptismal consecration as "kings," or *stewards* of the kingship of Christ. The

---

[1]See *General Instruction on the Roman Missal*, 2002; henceforth *GIRM*, nos. 80-88.
[2]See *Revelation* 19:9. This text gives the theme of the *Rite of Communion*.
[3]*Ephesians* 1:10. This is the new *American Bible* (1970) version.

Rite of Communion gives us the hope we need to persevere as "faithful stewards," working to establish the Kingdom until Christ comes again.

The soul of stewardship is *responsibility*. By Baptism we are committed and empowered to take responsibility for establishing the reign of God's peace and love over every area and activity of human life until Christ comes again. We are responsible for everything, from ecology to economics to ecumenism.

This seems a hopeless undertaking. What will it take to transform and renew family life, social customs, education, the prison system, health care, business, politics, the Church, everything that is either a root or fruit of human culture?

That is the key word: *culture*. We are called, consecrated, and sent, not just to convert individual human beings, but to transform human culture.

> For the Church it is a question not only of preaching the Gospel in ever wider geographic areas or to ever greater numbers of people, but also of affecting and as it were upsetting, through the power of the Gospel, humankind's criteria of judgment, determining values, points of interest, lines of thought, sources of inspiration, and models of life, which are in contrast with the Word of God and the plan of salvation....
>
> *What matters is to evangelize human culture and cultures*, not in a purely decorative way, as it were, by applying a thin veneer, but in a vital way, in depth and right to their very roots.[4]

The task is not hopeless, because it has already been achieved. In "God's time" Christ has won. Jesus declared victory on the eve of his apparent defeat on the cross:

> I have said this to you, so that in me you may have peace. In the world you face persecution. But take courage; *I have conquered the world!*"[5]

In the *Rite of Communion* we celebrate his victory. More than that, we experience in anticipation the "peace and unity of his kingdom" in a preview of the "wedding banquet of the Lamb." This is a "mystical experience"—a conscious awareness of being in touch with the

---

[4]Paul VI, *Evangelization in the Modern World*, nos. 19-20. And see no. 70: the task of the *laity*.
[5]*John* 16:33.

70

mystery of Christ's triumph. This renews our hope and gives us motivation to keep working to establish the Kingdom.

In the Lord's Prayer a petition is made for daily food,
which for Christians means preeminently the Eucharistic bread...[6]

The *Rite of Communion* begins with the *Our Father*. All of its petitions are asking for the "end time" when Christ will return in glory and the goal of his mission will be perfectly achieved.

Because of its position, when the *Our Father* is recited in the Mass it has a tone of celebrating these petitions as already accomplished. As such, it serves as the perfect introduction to our entrance into the "end time" in the *Rite of Communion*. We have "remembered" (and made present) Christ's redemptive death, resurrection, and ascension during the *Eucharistic Prayer*. Now we rejoice in the fruits of his victory.

The petitions of the *Our Father* sum up the basic mysteries of Christianity and Baptism that we have focused on in the Mass so far:[7]

The first petition: *"Father in heaven, hallowed be thy name"* asks for the day when the Father will be known and loved by all of redeemed humanity as he is in himself; that is, not only as Creator but as *Father*. This is the fulfillment of God's "plan for the fullness of time, to gather up all things in Christ," when "all of us [will have] become one in faith and in the knowledge of God's Son, and form that perfect man who is Christ come to full stature." This is the *first mystery of Baptism*: that by sharing in the gift of divine life, the "grace of our Lord Jesus Christ, we all "become Christ," and in him "sons and daughters of the Father." It is for this *new identity* that we give God praise and thanksgiving in the *Introductory Rites*.[8]

---

[6]*GIRM*, no. 81.
[7]See the *Catechism of the Catholic Church*, nos. 2759 to 2865; especially 2771-2772, 2788, 2796, 2804. The explanation that follows relies on Fr. Raymond Brown's "The *Pater Noster* As An Eschatological Prayer" in *New Testament Essays*, Bruce Publishing Co., 1965; republished by Doubleday, Image Books, 1968.
[8]*Ephesians* 1:10; 4:13; *Acts* 2:41. See *Catechism of the Catholic Church*, nos. 795-796; 2782-2784; 2813-2815.

When we pray, *"hallowed be thy name,"* we are praying for universal *enlightenment*, asking that we and the whole world will know and love the Father, and, by knowing him more and more perfectly, will grow into the fullness of the divine life we have received. Jesus said, "This is eternal life, that they may *know you,* the only true God, and Jesus Christ whom you have sent." This petition implants in us more deeply the desire to "devote ourselves to the apostles' teaching" and to enter into *the second mystery of Baptism: enlightenment* as *disciples* in the *Liturgy of the Word.*[9]

The second petition: *"Thy Kingdom come!"* asks for God's reign to be established within every heart and throughout the world. This was the "headline proclamation" in the preaching of both John the Baptizer and Jesus: "The time is fulfilled, and the kingdom of God has come near. Repent, and believe in the good news." By the very fact of asking for this, we dedicate ourselves to making it happen. This petition is the cry of our commitment to continuing the *mission* of Jesus. This commitment is in itself an experience of faith and hope in the "gift of the Spirit," without whose empowering presence, such a mission would be unthinkable. We express our mature acceptance of all this in the *Presentation of Gifts,* which affirms *the third mystery of Baptism,* our *call* and *empowerment* as *prophets* pledged to bear *witness* to the Good News.[10]

The third petition: *"Thy will be done on earth as it is in heaven"* reminds us that God's will does not always appear so evidently good and desirable to us on earth as it does to God in heaven. Jesus himself experienced this in the garden of Gethsemane, when it cost him blood and tears to say to the Father, *"Your will be done."* We recoil, as Peter did, before the human pain of redemption through the cross. But to share with Jesus in the work of redemption we must accept *the fourth mystery of Baptism,* our baptismal consecration to give life as "*priests* in the Priest and victims in the Victim." We do this by uniting ourselves to Jesus in his sacrifice during the *Eucharistic Prayer,* offering our bodies as a "living sacrifice"; surrendering our "flesh for the life of the world" to let Jesus *express himself* through

---

[9]*John* 17:3.

[10]*Matthew* 3:2; 4:17; *Mark* 1:5; *Luke* 4:43. See *Catechism of the Catholic Church,* nos. 2818, 2819.

our physical words and actions. This is a true "dying to self." And it is *ministry*.[11]

The fourth and fifth petitions are looking forward to the "end time," asking for the Bread of the heavenly banquet, the "wedding banquet of the Lamb": *"Give us this day our [future] Bread."* This Bread is Jesus himself, the joy of the wedding feast, our joy here and hereafter, now and forever. In this petition and the next: *"Forgive us our trespasses as we forgive..."* we are focusing all our desire on union with—on knowledge, love, and enjoyment of—Jesus himself. Jesus is our daily desire. This is all we live for.

But union with Jesus is not an individualistic, one-on-one relationship. We ask for *union* with Jesus in *communion* with the rest of humanity, with all the other members of his redeemed body, both on earth and in heaven. This will be a reality only when *forgiveness* will be complete; when the Father is *"forgiving us our trespasses"* while *"we forgive"* one another as completely as he does. This is a necessary requirement, because heaven is a communal beatitude. The image Jesus used to describe it is a banquet. We pray for that banquet to come, and in these two petitions, center our desires every day on its two components: *union* with Jesus, the Bread of Life, and *communion* with others in perfect, universal forgiveness and reconciliation: the "peace and unity" of the Kingdom. This puts our focus on the "end time" and on the *fifth mystery of Baptism*: our consecration as *kings* or *stewards* of the kingship of Christ.

Our dedication to mission as *prophets* and our surrender as *priests* to ministry now culminate in *total abandonment* of all we are and have to the work of establishing the reign of God on earth in the image of what it will be in heaven. We live to be *stewards* of his kingship.

The sixth and seventh petitions: *"And lead us not into temptation* (or "into hard testing"; "subject us not to the trial") *but deliver us from evil"* recognize that evil does not give up without a struggle—especially a final struggle against the final and total triumph of the "grace of our Lord Jesus Christ."

---

[11]*Matthew* 16:21-22 and 26:42. See *Catechism of the Catholic Church*, nos. 2824, 2825.

This triumph takes place on both the individual and cosmic levels. On the cosmic level the victory is called the *"Parousia,"* Christ's return in glory. On the individual level it is called the "grace of final perseverance," and consists essentially in saying "Yes" to death, leaving all we experience as life on this earth and abandoning ourselves willingly, with faith, hope, and love made perfect, into the hands of the Father: "Father, into your hands I commend my spirit."[12]

In the "Lord's Prayer" we recall Christ's priorities and not only affirm them as our own, but affirm our faith that they have been won by his victory on the cross.

> *The [presider] alone adds the embolism....*
> *Enlarging upon the last petition of the Lord's Prayer, [it]*
> *begs deliverance from the power of evil....*

An "embolism" is "something inserted." Here it is a prayer inserted between the *Our Father* and the *Rite of Peace*. What it does is repeat, in reverse order, all the petitions of the *Our Father*, addressing them now to the "Lord." Jesus has won the victory, and he is in a position to grant us what he came to establish. So, repeating the last petition, we say:

"Deliver us, Lord, from every evil." After ending the *Our Father* with "Lead us not into temptation [subject us not to the trial] but *deliver us from evil"* (*a malo*), we repeat the petition in the plural: "from all evils" (*ab omnibus malis*). Jesus has overcome all evil. He can deliver us.

"Graciously grant peace in our days" is a chorus to *"Forgive us our trespasses as we forgive...."* We pray for the "peace and unity" of the Kingdom, won by Jesus, the "sacrificial Victim, by whose death God was pleased to reconcile to himself all things... by making peace through the blood of his cross." Peace is won. In the "wedding banquet of the Lamb" all will be forgiven as they are forgiven.[13]

The petition *"Give us...bread"* is not echoed; possibly because it is the central petition and theme of the *Rite of Communion*. Everything

---

[12]*Luke* 23:46. Some unite these and count six petitions in the *Our Father*. For "final perseverance" see *Catechism of the Catholic Church*, no. 2849. For "Deliver us" see 2851, 2853. For *Parousia* see the *Reflection* for the Thirty-second Sunday below.
[13]*Colossians* 1:20-22; *Eucharistic Prayer III*.

leads to and is realized in the "wedding banquet of the Lamb," where the food of the banquet is Jesus, Bread of Life.

"...*That, by the help of your mercy, we may be always free from sin and safe from all distress...*" is a prayer that would not make sense if Jesus could not bring it about that the Father's *"will be done on earth as it is in heaven."* We can never be "free of sin" and "safe from all distress" so long as we or anyone else still acts against the Father's will. We ask Jesus for it because Jesus has made it happen. God has "put all things in subjection under his feet..... When all things are subjected to him, then the Son himself will also be subjected to the one who put all things in subjection under him, so that God may be All in all." Through his victory, Jesus has made "thy will be done" the permanent state of the world.[14]

"As we await the blessed hope and the manifestation of the glory of our great God and Savior, Jesus Christ" is a declaration of faith that the petition, *"Thy kingdom come,"* has already been realized. Jesus reigns, seated at the right hand of the Father. He has "made us to be a kingdom, priests serving his God and Father, to him be glory and dominion forever and ever. Amen." In our earthly time-frame we still await his coming. But the Kingdom is won.

There were loud voices in heaven, saying, "The kingdom of the world has become the kingdom of our Lord and of his Messiah, and he will reign forever and ever."[15]

He can say to us now, "I confer on you, just as my Father has conferred on me, a kingdom." We await his return.[16]

"For the kingdom, the power, and the glory are yours, now and forever" converts the petition *"Hallowed be thy name"* into a proclamation. It is done. Jesus can say to the Father: "I glorified you on earth by finishing the work that you gave me to do. It is finished."

Jesus came that we might "have life and have it to the full." He defined this fullness of life as knowing the Father: "And this is eternal life, that they may know you, the only true God, and Jesus Christ whom you have sent." Now it is done. Jesus has revealed the Father

---

[14] *1Corinthians* 15:28.
[15] *Revelation* 1:6; 11:15.
[16] *Luke* 22:29.

to all who believe. *Hallowed is his name.* "*The kingdom, the power, and the glory are yours, now.*" And forever.[17]

The "Lord's Prayer" introduces our celebration of the "end time" by listing the victories within Christ's victory. The "embolism" repeats them in ascending order of triumph. Jesus *delivers us from evil* as the Lamb of God who "takes away the sins of the world," that we might be *forgiven and forgiving* as we are nourished by the *daily bread* of his own Body and Blood. As the taste and desire for this impel us to say "*thy will be done*" in all our dealings with others, we will see the peace and unity of the *kingdom* realized in our time. Then the Father's name will be *hallowed*. The *kingdom, the power, and the glory* will be manifestly his, *now and forever*.

> *The Rite of Peace follows, by which the Church asks for peace and unity for herself and for the whole human family, and the faithful express to each other their ecclesial communion and mutual charity before communicating in the Sacrament.*

"Peace" is the word most frequently used (seven times) in the *Rite of Communion*. It was the greeting, gift, and promise the victorious Jesus bestowed on those to whom he appeared after his resurrection. Through Jesus "God was pleased to reconcile to himself all things, whether on earth or in heaven, by making peace through the blood of his cross."

"Peace" was the greeting Jesus instructed his disciples to give when they announced the Good News, and it appears in the salutation of every letter Paul wrote. Paul named it as a "fruit of the Spirit." It was Jesus' parting promise to his apostles at the Last Supper. "Peace and joy" are characteristic of the Kingdom of God, and the "peace and unity" of his Kingdom will prevail in the "end time" at the "wedding banquet of the Lamb."[18]

The "Sign of peace" is not a simple declaration of fellowship or of mutual forgiveness. It is an *eschatological* gesture. It is less an expression of what we are doing right now than an expression of what we believe Jesus is doing right now and will bring to perfection when

---

[17]*John* 10:10; 17:3; 19:28-30. And see *Matthew* 11:27; *John* 14:7-9.
[18]*Luke* 24:36; *John* 20:19, 21, 26. *Matthew* 10:13; *Luke* 10:5; *John* 14:27; 16:33; *Colossians* 1:20; *Galatians* 5:22; *Romans* 14:17.

he "comes again." It is a gesture of faith and hope that focuses us on the "end time."

We are not really saying to the persons to whom we give the sign of peace, "All is well between us." In some cases that would be hypocrisy. Rather, we are professing our faith that one day all *will be* well between us. We may not be ready for complete reconciliation now; but we are saying we believe Christ can and will bring it about; that we desire it, are open to it, and know that we won't have a place in the "wedding banquet of the Lamb" until we are forgiving each other as perfectly as God forgives us. The "Sign of Peace" is a sign of faith that Jesus who said, "Peace I leave you, my peace I give you," will in fact, "look not on our sins, but on the faith of the Church," and "graciously grant" to her and to the whole human race, by the overwhelming power of his victory over sin, death, and division, that "peace and unity" that are in accordance with his will.

The [presider] breaks the Eucharistic Bread....
Christ's gesture of breaking bread at the Last Supper,
which gave the entire Eucharistic Action its name
in apostolic times, signifies that the many faithful
are made one body by receiving Communion from
the one Bread of Life which is Christ.

Immediately after the Sign of Peace the liturgy echoes a verse from the *Gloria*: "Lamb of God, you take away the sins of the world, have mercy on us."

In the *Introductory Rites* this is a chant of evangelization and identification. In the *Rite of Communion* it is a song of triumph. The message is the same, but the tone is different—like the difference between the angels proclaiming "peace on earth" as a promise at Christ's birth and Jesus bestowing "Peace!" as a blessing after his resurrection.

In the *Gloria* we proclaim Jesus as the "Lamb of God who takes away the sin of the world" quoting John the Baptizer, who proclaimed what Jesus would do. But in the *Rite of Communion*, when we proclaim him the "Lamb of God" we are conscious that what was promised has been accomplished. We have just celebrated in the *Eucharistic Prayer* the sacrifice by which the Lamb of God took on and took away the sins of the world. Now we are proclaiming him victorious over sin and death.

Then I looked, and I heard the voice of many angels surrounding the throne and the living creatures and the elders... singing with full voice, "Worthy is the Lamb that was slaughtered to receive power and wealth and wisdom and might and honor and glory and blessing!... Salvation belongs to our God who is seated on the throne, and to the Lamb!"...

"Now have come the salvation and the power and the kingdom of our God and the authority of his Messiah, for the accuser of our comrades has been thrown down.... They have conquered him by the blood of the Lamb and by the word of their testimony, for they did not cling to life even in the face of death."[19]

In the *Gloria* we said, "You take away the sins of the world, receive our prayer." In the *Rite of Communion* we ask him, as one empowered by his victory to answer all prayers, his and ours—not just to "have mercy" but to "grant us peace," the total peace of the Kingdom he came to establish.

While the assembly is singing the *Agnus Dei*, the presider "breaks the Eucharistic Bread." This is the gesture Jesus made at the Last Supper and again with the disciples he met on the road to Emmaus: "When he was at the table with them, he *took* bread, *blessed* and *broke* it, and *gave* it to them.

These four words—"took," "blessed" (or "gave thanks"), "broke," and "gave"—became the identifying formula for Eucharist. It is the use of this formula that tells us the miracle of the "multiplication of the loaves" was meant as a preview of Eucharist. It is because of this combination that we know it was in Eucharist that the disciples' "eyes were opened, and they recognized him," and could report later "how he had been made known to them in the breaking of the bread."[20]

This gesture "signifies that the many faithful are made one body by receiving Communion from the one Bread of Life which is Christ." That is why the loaf or host the presider handles should be big enough to be visibly broken and shared with the assembly. In the same way, the chalice from which the presider receives the blood of Christ should be shared with the assembly.

The cup of blessing that we bless, is it not a sharing in the blood of Christ? The bread that we break, is it not a sharing in the body of Christ? Because

---

[19]*Revelation* 5:11-12; 7:10; 12:10-11.
[20]See *Matthew* 14:19; 15:36; 26:26; *Mark* 6:41; 8:6; *Luke* 9:16; 22:19; 24:30-31; *1Corinthians* 11:23-26.

there is one bread, we who are many are one body, for we all partake of the one bread.[21]

It is important that we should look around and see that all are being nourished by the one Bread. All are receiving from Jesus Christ the same sign of affirmation and love. "*Take this, all of you*, and eat of it... This is my Body... given up for you."

In the "breaking of the bread" we see that we all are one, that we all have the same divine value in the eyes of God.

> *The [presider] next shows the faithful the Eucharistic Bread,*
> *holding it above the paten or above the chalice,*
> *and invites them to the [wedding] banquet of [the Lamb].*

There are three "elevations" in the Mass: times when the presider "shows the faithful the Eucharistic Bread." The "elevations" focus us, successively, on "Christ has died; Christ is risen; Christ will come again."

In the host and chalice, Christ is present simultaneously as offering himself on the cross, as rising from the dead, and as reigning at the right hand of the Father until he returns in glory. In God's time these are all one moment, like the "hour" of Christ in the Gospels. But in our time we need to focus on them one at a time.[22]

The first elevation takes place during the *Institution Narrative*, when the presider lifts up the body and blood of Christ separated, as in death, saying in his name, "This is my body... This is my blood... given up for you... poured out for you." The focus is on "Christ has died."

In the second elevation, at the end of the *Eucharistic Prayer*, the presider lifts up the body and blood of Christ together, as reunited, and we focus on the *risen* Jesus present in the host and present in all the people who are his risen body on earth. Now the presider proclaims that if we, his risen body in the world, act *"through him and with him and in him, in the unity of the Holy Spirit,"* we will give *"all honor and glory"* to the Father *"for ever and ever."* The focus is on "Christ is risen."

---

[21] *1Corinthians* 10:16-17.
[22] *Matthew* 24:36, 45; *Mark* 14:35, 41; *Luke* 12:40; 22:53; *John* 2:4; 5:28; 7:30; 8:20; 12:23; 13:1; 17:1.

In the third elevation the presider "shows the faithful the Eucharistic Bread, holding it above the paten or above the chalice, and invites them to the banquet of Christ." These words of the *Instruction* echo the previous translation used in the liturgy, which was, "Happy are those who are called to his supper." The new translation more faithfully translates the Latin text, which is, "Blessed are those called to the supper of the Lamb." This is a word-for-word quotation from St. Jerome's Latin Vulgate translation of the *Book of Revelation* 19:9, except that it edits out one word: *nuptiarum*. The true words of Scripture are, "Blessed are those who are invited to the *marriage* supper of the Lamb."

This is not just any supper. The context is the end of the world. The Lamb is before the throne. John sees the Church, "the holy city, the new Jerusalem, coming down out of heaven from God, prepared as a bride adorned for her husband." The "end time" is described as a wedding banquet; the "marriage supper of the Lamb."

> Then I heard what seemed to be the voice of a great multitude, like the sound of many waters and like the sound of mighty thunder peals, crying out, "Hallelujah! For the Lord our God the Almighty reigns. Let us rejoice and exult and give him the glory, for the marriage of the Lamb has come, and his bride has made herself ready; to her it has been granted to be clothed with fine linen, bright and pure"....
>
> And the angel said to me, "Write this: *Blessed are those who are invited to the marriage supper of the Lamb.*"[23]

This is the Church's defiant shout in the face of every threat, persecution, and death itself: *"Blessed are those who are invited to the marriage supper of the Lamb!"* Christ has conquered. The Lamb has overcome sin and death. The victory is won. The wedding banquet has begun. We are invited. The worst our enemies can do by killing us is project us into the party!

---

[23]*Revelation* 19:7-9; 21:2, 9; 22:17. The previous translation left out the word "Lamb," without which we do not know we are in the "end time" of the *Book of Revelation*. The present translation leaves out the word "marriage" (or "wedding"), without which we lose the biblical imagery that presents Christ as Bridegroom and the Church as Bride. And we lose connection with the whole concept of spousal love for Christ, without which we cannot begin to understand the mystics; for example, John of the Cross and Teresa of Avila. Fortunately, the new translation does give the authentic text in a footnote. See also *Matthew* 9:15; 22:2-12; 25:1-10; *John* 2:1-11; 3:29; *Ephesians* 5:21-32; And see, for example, Teresa of Avila: *Interior Castle*, Dwelling VII, chapters 1 and 2; St. John of the Cross: *Spiritual Canticle*, Theme (*Argumento*) 1.

Behold the Lamb of God!
Behold him who takes away the sins of the world!
Blessed are those who are invited to the marriage supper of the Lamb.

*The Communion chant is begun. Its purpose is to express
the communicants' union in spirit
by means of the unity of their voices, to show joy of heart,
and to highlight more clearly the "communitarian" nature
of the procession to receive Communion.*

Before the Vatican Council's reform of the liturgy we were taught to process up to receive Communion, conscious only of Jesus and ourselves. Communion was a deep, personal, and private moment between God and each one of us. To look around or to sing a hymn at this moment would have been a distraction.

Communion should still be deep and personal; but not private. The *Instruction* tells us to sing, to "show joy of heart," to make visible the "communitarian nature" of the procession to receive Communion. Receiving Communion is about as private as Thanksgiving dinner. (In the United States, Thanksgiving is the day of the year that, more than any other, draws families together). The Church wants the receiving of Communion to look as much as possible like a family meal. Because, first and foremost, that is what it is.

The *Instruction* told us above that "Christ's gesture of *breaking bread* at the Last Supper... gave the entire Eucharistic Action its name in apostolic times." The words "breaking bread" were a common expression for eating together that the early Christians employed when speaking of the Mass.[24]

---

[24]The *Jerome Biblical Commentary* (1968) says about the phrase "breaking of the bread" in *Acts* 2:42: "Eucharistic overtones in this community meal are hard to deny (cf. *Luke* 24:30, 35)... In fact, Luke seems not to distinguish the Eucharist and the common meal.... The ideal first community enjoyed table-fellowship with those who were privileged table-fellows of the Risen One (cf. 1:4; 10:41). Paul's followers will later have the same fellowship with him as a successor to the Twelve (20:7)." In the *New JBC* (1990) the same author writes: "Originally the ritual opening of a festive Jewish meal, this was the gesture of the Risen One at Emmaus and recalls the earlier dominical instructions with bread-breaking as well (*Luke* 9:11-27; 22:14-38). We can consider the phrase a [technical term] for the Eucharist in Luke-Acts."

In our day, with large numbers at Mass lining up to receive from a handful of Eucharistic ministers, the Communion procession has the appearance (distasteful to even think about) of people going up to a vending machine to get their sandwich, then going back to their places to eat it alone as isolated individuals. The Church tells us to do the best we can to counter this impression. One way is to sing while going up to receive Communion, because singing expresses "union of spirit."

Another way is to make a point of *looking around* at others who are receiving. We should do this conscious that we are seeing each other precisely as people invited to eat at the "table of the Lord." People whom Jesus himself is feeding. He is putting into each one's hands the bread that he has blessed and broken and is now giving to each as the Bread of Life, his own body and blood. This should make us feel differently about one another. Communion is a preview of the "wedding banquet of the Lamb." At this moment we should see everyone as perfect; see all as we will be when Christ "presents the Church to himself in splendor, without a spot or wrinkle or anything of the kind—yes... holy and without blemish." Communion is a time to see one another with new eyes. Eyes of faith, open to mystery.[25]

When the distribution of Communion is finished...
the [presider] and faithful spend some time praying privately.

There is a time to enclose ourselves privately with Christ. After all have received and the procession is over, the *Instruction* directs that the assembly "may sit or kneel while the period of sacred silence after Communion is observed."

After all have received, we stop singing. We "enclose ourselves" deeply with Jesus present within us. The experience of receiving him physically in Communion helps us enter into the ongoing mystery of his constant, spiritual presence in us by grace.

By the gift of grace, God unites himself to us and us to him "on the level of being." We need to understand what this admittedly abstract, philosophical phrase is saying. It is saying that we are united with

---

[25] *Ephesians* 5:27.

God in a way that is only possible with him. On a level deeper than the union we can have with any other person or creature.

With other people we can only be united on the level of *operation*. We can carry a box together; or carry on a conversation. We are united in the action of communicating with each other; of understanding the same truth with our intellects, or embracing the same goal or ideal with our wills. But we don't share in each other's *being*. What we call "sharing each other's life" really means sharing in what we both *do*. And what we do together is always a blend, a combination of two separate actions, of two separate persons working together.

But with God, by grace, we are united precisely on the level of being, "prior to operation." We become one with Jesus in such a way that from Jesus and ourselves, united on the level of being, can proceed *one* operation, one action, that comes from the two of us. We are not united *by* the operation, through the fact of acting together. Rather, we are united *in* the operation, in producing together one and the same action that comes from the two of us united already on the level of being.

When we love by grace, there is only one act of love. Because it is our act, it is human. Because it is God's act, it is divine. Because we are united with God on the level of being, prior to operation, it is one divine-human act of love that is equally ours and God's. We are loving divinely as well as humanly; God is loving humanly as well as divinely; we are both united in one action of loving in a way that is both human and divine. What has this got to do with Communion?

In Communion, Jesus comes just to give us himself. Not to do anything.

In *Baptism*, he comes to incorporate us into his body and share his divine life with us. In *Reconciliation*, he comes to forgive and heal us. In *Confirmation*, he comes to empower us for mission by the Gift of the Holy Spirit. In *Matrimony* and *Holy Orders*, he comes to work with and within us to establish life-giving communities of love. In *Anointing of the Sick*, he comes to heal and strengthen us for our final act of total abandonment to God. But in *Communion*, he comes just to give us himself. As he does in heaven.

Communion is a preview, a foretaste of heaven.

This doesn't mean that in Communion we experience ecstasy or feel the joy we will feel in heaven. But we do experience, should experience, are invited to experience, the *awareness* of being united with Jesus, one with God, on the level of our deepest being. We know—and are invited to be consciously aware—that we have God himself within us. We are united to him on the level of our very being. We have as belonging to our being (and not just as the effect of a momentary operation) everything we need to be perfectly happy for all eternity. We have Life eternal. God's own Life. Within us. Ours.

It is not possible to directly *experience* this Life, or this presence of God within us, in any human way. We cannot perceive it with our senses. Or get in touch with it through our emotions. We cannot really *know* it with our intellects. And no matter what we do or choose with our wills, it does not give us the direct experience of union with God on the level of being. So what experience does Communion give us?

In *The Interior Castle*, St. Teresa of Avila says that "in the soul His Majesty must have a room where he dwells alone." This is the "very interior center of the soul." It is "where God Himself is, and… there is no need of any door for Him to enter."[26]

Teresa explains: "I say there is no need of any door, because everything that has been said up to now [about experiencing God in prayer] seems to take place by means of the senses and faculties" [through the intellectual thought process of meditation, for example]. But this dwelling of God in us is on a level too deep for our senses or faculties to reach. It is on the level of our very being.

God can give us feelings or put thoughts into our heads whenever he wishes, and he needs no permission from us to do this. But there is a depth, a level of our soul that God will not enter into in personal union unless we invite him. And when he is there, we cannot join him in any conscious or experiential way unless he brings us in by

---

[26]VII, ch. 1, no. 5.

an extraordinary gift of mystical prayer. This is the deep center of our souls, deeper than any sense, knowledge, or feeling, deeper than rational knowledge or thought. This is the level of our *being*, the level of existence that underlies all the levels of our activity, whether rational, emotional, or sensitive. This is a level that is deeper than thought or feeling. This is the level we are invited to be aware of "while the period of sacred silence after Communion is observed."[27]

Where God dwells within us is a "doorless room." But we can sit outside the door just being *aware* of what is inside. Aware that He-Who-Is is inside us. He is not saying anything (and we need not say anything to him). He is not doing anything (and not asking us to do anything either). He is just there. Giving us himself. And we are given to him. That is the preview of heaven.

Because it is a preview of heaven, it is not precisely true that in this time of silent awareness we "enclose ourselves privately with Christ." We do that, but with explicit awareness that we are not alone with him. We are sharing him together with all those present who are also united with him in Communion. We are at the "wedding banquet of the Lamb." It is a communal enjoyment, as heaven is.

We are aware in Communion that the "peace and unity" of the Kingdom is pervading this place. No one is acting. No one is arguing or fighting. No one is actively involved at this moment in any of the activities, pursuits, or undertakings that sometimes cause division between us. No one is doing anything. We are all just being with God. Present to God. Present to one another as we are mutually present to God.

It is a "time out." We are out of time and into eternity. Nothing exists for us now, during these few moments, except God and our-selves. Jesus and his body. All of us one with God and each other. We are at the "end time," when, in the words of St. Augustine, there "will be but one Christ, loving himself."[28]

Communion is a time just to experience love. And peace. And the foretaste of total fulfillment.

---

[27]*GIRM*, no. 43.
[28]Homily 10 on the First Epistle of John, no. 3.

> The wolf shall live with the lamb,
> the leopard shall lie down with the kid...
> and the lion shall eat straw like the ox....
> They will not hurt or destroy on all my holy mountain;
> for the earth will be full of the knowledge of the LORD
> as the waters cover the sea.[29]

This is the experience; this is the foretaste that motivates us to go out from Mass and work for the Kingdom of God. Holy Communion is a launching pad that propels us into persevering efforts to "renew the face of the earth." The *Rite of Communion* impels us to *stewardship*.

---

[29]*Isaiah* 11:6-9.

Questions for Reflection and Discussion

- How does the *Rite of Communion* make the mystery of the "end time" real as present and impacting my life right now?
- Can I accept and claim this as a "mystical experience"?
- To what are we consecrated and committed by our baptismal anointing as *stewards* of the kingship of Christ?
- What are we asking for in all of the petitions of the *Our Father*?
- What are we expressing in the *Sign of Peace*?
- What should the "breaking of the bread" make us aware of?
- Why are the words of the "third elevation" a "defiant shout"?
- Why do we sing during the Communion procession?
- Why should we look around while everyone is receiving Communion?
- What should we do during the period of sacred silence after Communion?
- Why is Communion a preview, a foretaste of heaven?

Key Points: What can I say now about:

The celebration of the "end time" at Mass?

The *Rite of Communion* as a motivation to faithful *stewardship*?

The *Our Father* and the role it plays in the *Rite of Communion*?

The "three elevations" at Mass?

The *Sign of Peace* as an "eschatological gesture"?

The "communitarian nature" of the procession to receive Communion?

Father David Knight has spent 50 years of priesthood ministering as a pastor, high school teacher, professor of theology, missioner, and retreat director. He lives in Memphis, TN, and runs His Way Center for Spiritual Growth. Father Knight teaches in the Christian Brothers University Graduate Program in Catholic Studies and the Diocese of Memphis Institute for Liturgy and Spirituality. He is retired as pastor of Sacred Heart Catholic Church.